RUSTIC REVISITED

"I BELIEVE IN GOD, ONLY I SPELL IT IN NATURE."

Frank Lloyd Wright

RUSTIC
REVISITED

INNOVATIVE DESIGN
FOR CABIN, CAMP, AND LODGE

ANN STILLMAN O'LEARY

PHOTOGRAPHS BY ANDREW WELLMAN

WATSON-GUPTILL PUBLICATIONS NEW YORK

EDITORIAL DIRECTOR: VICTORIA CRAVEN
PROJECT EDITOR: MARTHA MORAN
DESIGNER: ALEXANDRA MALDONADO
PRODUCTION MANAGER: HECTOR CAMPBELL

First published in 2006 by Watson-Guptill Publications,
a division of VNU Business Media, Inc.,
770 Broadway, New York, N.Y. 10003
www.wgpub.com

Library of Congress Cataloging-in-Publication Data

O'Leary, Ann Stillman.
Rustic revisited : innovative design for cabin, camp, and lodge / Ann Stillman
O'Leary ; photographs by Andrew Wellman.
p. cm.
Includes index.
ISBN-13: 978-0-8230-4623-2
ISBN-10: 0-8230-4623-0
1. Country homes. 2. Interior architecture. 3. Decoration and ornament, Rustic.
I. Wellman, Andrew. II. Title.

NA7560.O44 2006
728.7--dc22

Manufactured in China

First printing, 2006

1 2 3 4 5 6 7 8 9 / 14 13 12 11 10 09 08 07 06

Thank you to all whose photographs and renderings are in this book:
Andrew Wellman; stacey brandford photography; Chicken Coop Forge;
John Cottle; Crystal Farm, Mark Darley/Esto; Billy Doran; Greg Faulkner; Fletcher
Farr Ayotte, Inc.; Nick Gorski/NKG Studios; gordongregoryphoto.com; The Great
Camp Collection; Barry Gregson; Gary Hall Photography;
Larry Hawkins; maxhaynes.com; Mark Hobson; Jared Hoke; David Horton; Lean-to
Studio; Charles Lindsay and Shope, Reno, Wharton Associates; Midnight Farms;
Mill Creek Post & Beam; Robert Millman Photography; Pendleton Woolen Mills; Bill
Perkins; RKD; Warren Roos; Ron Ruscio Photography; SALA; Durston Saylor; Jack
Snow; Cheryle St. Onge; Paul Stark; Ginny Stine Interiors, Doug Tedrow; Dino Tonn
Photography, Matt Turley Photographer; Peter Vitale; Roger Wade; Ryan A.
Wolffe/Shepherd Resources, Inc.

A dedication to the sisterhood of women whose strength and support empowered me to survive life's challenges during the writing of this book: my deceased mother Eileen, sisters Julie and Martha, daughter Martha, and all of the Marthas before them. My sisters at heart: Margie, Nia, Valerie, Tracey, Sheila, Janice, Joann, Cindy, Susan, J.P., Erin, and Paige, and all of the women past, present, and future whose presence has graced my life.

I would like to acknowledge the generosity of the homeowners who opened their doors and allowed us to have the run of their homes. Hats off to the talented architects, interior designers, builders, and craftsmen who rose to the occasion and created compelling, good designs; I hope we have "done them all proud." My sister, agent, and editor, Julie Stillman, who championed this project, taking great care through the publishing process to keep it intact and, more importantly, insure its completion. Many thanks to Sara Hart for her astute and insightful guidance in defining the subject at hand; Judy Brown of Bounds Cave Rugs who became our friend and ambassador for the state of North Carolina; computer wonderboy Zac Burger for retrieving my manuscript from cyberspace; and Dave Gitto for his expertise on stone.

I am truly indebted to Diane Miller, my assistant, who has held our office together, weathered a tempest, and put up the good front for me when I was beyond it.

Bless you all.

Rocky Mountain Ski House—Colorado

CONTENTS

Architect Jim Taylor was inspired by the work of Bernard Maybeck, whose elaborate paneling has been reinterpreted to become the defining element of this great room in the Adirondacks.

© Gary Hall Photography

PREFACE

Until I moved to the Adirondacks in 1989, I spent most of my life living in suburban or urban settings. At one time or another I have lived in a colonial home, a farmhouse, a Victorian beach house, and a skyscraper. These were familiar and expected forms dressed in the predictable surfaces: clapboard, cedar shake, and concrete. I was caught off guard by the first rustic home I saw, a remarkable camp on Lake George in the Adirondack Mountains designed by the venerable firm Bohlin Cywinski Jackson. It was unexpected, a curiosity; it required thought. There were recognizable features but the details and proportions had been tweaked. The overscale and purposely precarious stone foundation rose from the site like a prehistoric wall, hyperbolic spaces were amplified by towering tree columns, and light fixtures were expressed in contemporized sled and snowshoe shapes. It was a modernist's take on the traditional Great Camp. Over the next few years I recognized that a rustic renaissance was taking place, and documented this in my book *Adirondack Style* published in 1998. *Rustic Revisited* gives a fuller account, traveling beyond the Adirondack style and taking a look at the evolution of rustic architecture across the continent. The revival of this style, popular for over 100 years, is seeing many new, important structures built by a new generation of architects.

There are no typical rustic homes; they come in many guises: a prairie cabin, a shingle-style cottage, a twig-encrusted Great Camp, a peeled-log western lodge. The elements of nature define these structures; the building materials are used unrefined and are often taken from the site itself. They are made from stone, log, branches, and bark in their most primitive state. Sara Hart, Senior Editor at *Architectural Record* magazine comments, "Rustic has appeal as the antidote to the hardness of concrete, the glossiness of steel, urban dwellings or the blandness of suburbia." On a more visceral level rustic design appeals to a generation of baby boomers who hold fond memories of summer camp, a family vacation in the woods, a dude ranch, or simply, the tree house in the backyard. A rustic home fulfills a dream for overworked achievers; it is a deserved departure and a reclaiming of youth. Inherently the shapes are lively, the details lighthearted, and the rules beg to be broken.

Some rustic homes are designed to reflect the owner's comfort with the past and are references to homes built over a century ago. Others merely use historic precedent as a jumping-off point, boldly redefining rustic for the 21st century. All of them seek to meld the rustic with the luxurious, integrating modern convenience with the vernacular of the style.

Locations for these homes tend to be rugged settings, typically mountain, lake, or cliff side. Their visages are expressed in the Adirondack Camp style, North Woods architecture of the Midwest, mountain homes of the South, coastal and inland houses of the Pacific Northwest, and the contrasting architecture of the New and Old West.

It is safe to say that remarkable rustic dwellings have been built in every state across our country. From a Great Camp in the Adirondacks that has been transformed into a rustic wonderland to a futuristic home in Colorado, each stands alone and all represent the best of what rustic has become during its revival over the last two decades.

Rustic Revisited examines the key elements of rustic design, and takes a tour of 30 exceptional homes, each speaking the rustic dialect of its region and exemplifying a vision shared by owner, architect, and interior designer. The country's leading rustic artisans are featured throughout and the last chapter is a guide to rustic decoration, from furniture to fabrics.

As an interior designer who specializes in rustic, I was sure I'd seen it all. Happily, I had not. In writing this book I was privileged to have entree to properties that were extraordinarily diverse, thought provoking, and otherwise inaccessible. I believe that this is the first book addressing the topic in a broader sense, connecting the dots, so to speak. In doing so I believe we have created a beautiful tribute to one of the quirkier and more colorful categories of North American architecture. Enjoy the tour!

The Warren "picnic cabin" built in 1934 was renovated recently. True to its Carolina roots, the original cabin was constructed of round native chestnut logs with a saddle-notched edge. This type of joinery is more authentic to the area than the square log currently favored in the newer homes in this area. The latter is recognized as a Tennessee feature and has been adopted here as well.

Built in 1912 as a summer home for Oregon Governor Oswald West, this log cabin was destroyed by fire in 1991. Working from historic photos and building plans, architects Fletcher Farr Ayotte designed the new structure to match the historic character of the original cabin. The privately owned property is on the National Register of Historic Places and appears on the National Park Service website as an exemplary reconstruction project.

Photograph courtesy Fletcher Farr Ayotte, Inc.

WHAT IS RUSTIC DESIGN?
AN OVERVIEW OF THE STYLE

We are only now defining this legitimate style of American architecture that remains unaddressed by the official architecture community. In order to label a type of architecture there has to be a number of examples of the style to make it a movement. I feel there are enough illustrations and permutations of rustic design across the country that it deserves to be added to future architectural surveys and critiques as a legitimate style. In labeling this genre, I have attempted to identify the common elements, the history, and the regional interpretations, all of which make rustic a distinct and distinguished style of its own.

RUSTIC DEFINED

The dictionary definition of rustic remains unsatisfactory; terms like "lacking elegance," "simple," and "artless" are inaccurate and don't do justice to this tribute to nature at the hands of man. It is hard to find an acceptable definition of this style that has been so well documented in the past decade. In putting rustic under the microscope, it's none of the above, and truly the opposite of those unflattering terms. Today's rustic is not the spartan cabin on Walden Pond, it is a design that celebrates the honesty of all-natural, local materials and brings them to new heights. Anything but simple, it can be the most complex of forms—a tangled web of willow or gnarled rhododendron root burl, that when molded with finesse can be fashioned into something masterful.

Rustic does not exist in architectural argot. As Sara Hart states, "The closest you'll get to a definition is 'rustication,' which can be a variety of bold textures on columns or facades, the inverse of honed, polished, or refined. Even in the most flattering light, rustic design is considered the architectural equivalent of folk art—emotional, eccentric, and personal. If we accept rustic as a modifier for lack of a better term, then perhaps the word itself, and the buildings it describes, need a semantic upgrade."

Rustic is the use of unprocessed materials kept as close as possible to their natural, uncultivated states and neighborhoods, with minimal exposure to machinery and technology. The closer a material is to its natural primitive condition, the more rustic it is. And, the fewer man-made substances—polymer, urethane, paint, and so forth—used to treat the natural material,

the truer it will be to its rustic roots.

As an architectural style, rustic falls under the category of "indigenous": structures built from local materials and designed to be responsive to the prevailing environmental and weather conditions. The Adirondack brand of rustic required the use of local materials because transporting supplies to this remote area was impractical. The deep overhangs of the Adirondack camps were intended to keep the snow and rain away from the foundations, a nod to the inclement weather in this region.

There may once have been a regional identity to rustic, but by and large the age of information has fomented a cross-breeding of styles. Words like "Mountdustrial" and "Colorondack," and Western ranches with heavy Adirondack overtones are telling. I imagine in the years to come rustic design may become less identifiable by region and more by architectural group. It will

A detail of the magnificent boathouse at Camp Topridge in the Adirondacks, where imagination was matched by skill. The maple leaf fascia detail is exceptional and is what makes this singular building one of the most outstanding in the Adirondacks. The architect's sketches were translated into full-sized stencils by craftsman Mike Trivieri and executed with a jigsaw by Chris McClusky of Tissot Construction.

become a generic rustic, an amalgam of styles. It's unfortunate that in an age of internet shopping and easy travel, many new rustic homes use materials shipped in from afar, diluting the regional flavor. The heritage of this building style is based upon a connection to the land and the locals who champion this rustic tradition.

Rustic is mostly about the materials, furnishings, and the aura of a space, not the physical space, floor plans, or fenestration, etc. It is how each builder or artisan manipulates the components that distinguishes one structure from the next. The craftsperson is not trying to imitate nature but respond to it, and each material used brings with it a set of options to consider. For example, when using logs: will the bark be on or off; will they be set with a flared root foot or straight cut; has bark been applied as skin or shingle? Will the stone be rough and ragged, pulled from the earth, or smoothed by river current? When using branches, roots, burls, pinecones, and acorns as embellishments, how will they fit together? Will antler or fur embellishments be used? For hand-hewn accent materials, what are the merits of iron and copper versus bronze? Each choice sends the project on a course that will give it its own identity. It is impossible to precisely duplicate nature, so no two rustic homes could be identical.

One universal trait of a rustic dwelling is the concept of "outside in." Many of the exterior finishes are brought inside—stonework foundations are invited in to act as wainscoting; slab siding becomes a wall product; natural forms such as trees and branches appear as leafless, sculptural forests throughout the house. With current technology, large undivided windows bring the outside in by providing seamless transitions. The idea is to feel as if you're living outdoors, or, welcoming it in as an integral part of the home.

RIGHT This master bath at Wildwood in Colorado is the epitome of a space that allows the outside in.
© Robert Millman Photography

BELOW A telescoping walkway, designed by architect Tim Greene, makes a clever bridge over an estuary at a home in the Smoky Mountains. The laurel balusters are interrupted by peeled locust posts— a typical rail treatment in the South. A veil of laurel branches has been applied as a decorative gable screen.

Rustic design is not a passing fancy. It has found a permanent home in the architectural vocabulary of North America, and like any legitimate style of building will be interpreted and reinterpreted by designers looking to advance the form and put their signatures on the category as it unfolds.

13

A HISTORY OF RUSTIC DESIGN

In the world of design, specifically architecture, the creative process does not occur in a vacuum. New design is in some way derived from a concept that has come before it. If we were to do a family tree of rustic architecture we'd see clearly what its lineage is. Of course rustic design began in prehistoric times, aptly named the Stone Age, when there was no other option but to use rustic materials. Moving on to more enlightened civilizations, the Chinese were recorded as building twig furniture over ten centuries ago (and have picked up the ball again to crank out container loads of what is acidly referred to as Chinarondack). Fast-forward 600 years to newly colonized America where, out of necessity and ingenuity, the Swedish built the first log cabins in Delaware in the 1630s. Moving along our continuum we witness the romantic and frivolous garden structures of Victorian England in the 1800s. A true, more palpable rustic design campaign began in the mid-to-late 1800s when the Picturesque Movement ignited interest in regionalism and the outdoors. In the Adirondack

RIGHT One of the most celebrated boathouses in the Adirondacks is the original boathouse at Topridge, which was built in the 1920s by Ben Muncil. The flared cedar columns and woven branchwork have been replicated in the new boathouse that sits adjacent to this.

OPPOSITE The National Park Service (NPS) structures were imaginative and widely varied, running the gamut from the simple rubble and log structure of the Madison Junction museum to the Casa Grande building patterned after Indian pueblos. They shared a common philosophy "spare no expense but keep it simple." This rustic frontier-style home designed by architect Larry Pearson and built by Yellowstone Traditions embodies another tenet of the NPS buildings, to "promote regional architecture by the use of native and historical materials and minimize the impact of the project on the existing landscape".

Photograph by gordongregoryphoto.com

Mountains hordes of thrill-seeking city folk made their way north for a wilderness experience. Their brush with nature likely involved some canoeing, picnicking, hiking, and plein-air sleeping in tents perched on platforms. In the late 1870s the first of the Adirondack Great Camps was built by William West Durant. Camp Pine Knot was well documented as a symphony in log, twig, and bark. This series of heavily twigged and barked cabins was the springboard for rustic architecture in the East. Majestic log lodges and compounds consisting of up to 64 structures were de rigueur for wealthy scions of industry, each camp striving to eclipse the last in a show of rustic peacockery. As this style fell out of favor during the Depression years the rustic dialogue was muted and decades of unfortunate knotty pine cabins and prefab vacation homes ensued.

Elsewhere, in the early years of the 20th century, national park hotels were built in the West for visitors to the newly accessible (via railroad) national parks. These lodges became the genesis of rustic architecture in the West. In the late 1920s,

the National Park Service picked up the torch and began a crusade to "physically improve" all of America's parks by adding roadside visitor facilities and patrol cabins. These non-intrusive structures, affectionately dubbed "Parkitecture," were built from all that the land had to offer; they are some of the finest examples of how rustic buildings can harmonize nature and man.

In the late 1990s, a generation of baby boomers with ample disposable income and aspirations for second homes renewed interest in resort areas: the Adirondacks, Blue Ridge Mountains, Tetons, Lake Muskoka, and other vacation destinations that spoke of summer camps, dude ranches, and childhoods remembered or coveted. They looked to the native styles and historic reference in these regions and designed their homes "in the manner of." The much-publicized renaissance of rustic architecture fueled the flames. Today the genre is alive and well and mutating. There are no fewer than 400,000 web sites at this writing that feature rustic architecture; it was a thin offering a decade ago.

REGIONAL RUSTIC

I was under the impression that historic models were influencing rustic architecture until I arrived in the West and discovered that there is a schism in the world of rustic architecture. In the East, South, and Midwest, traditionalism maintains a stronghold on rustic design. A deep comfort with the past and references to a gentler era drive the genre there. Homeowners in these regions tend to be establishment professionals, new money with old money aspirations. The use of conventional materials and long-established methods of construction pay homage to the past. The architects and interior designers of the more successful translations are true to the roots of rustic, they've done their homework and researched archives working to understand the origins of the style. In their study something may trigger a new translation of a natural element, keeping the spirit of experimentation alive. Many of these neoclassic rustic homes have a fresh attitude and exuberance yet are still based on tradition and do not trivialize the category.

Across the continent in the West, a different and prevailing wind blows. There is big imagery here, humbling mountain ranges, gargantuan logs, the lore of cowboys and Indians. But there is also an underlying current of modern. Contemporary mountain architecture, or the "New West" as it is being termed, is busting the cowboy myth wide open. Much of this emerging style is influenced by the team of client and architect and a willingness to hold hands and take a leap. Many of these clients are from regions that favor modern architecture, notably California. There is an ease and familiarity with

spare organic forms as well as the linear and an occasional industrial reference. The homes of Gehry and Neutra are not icons in this region but neighbors, contours not foreign to the local landscape. To close the gap, a number of architects are fusing the concepts in a convergence of the two wests. The West has become a laboratory for incorporating the principles of modern design with the elements of nature.

Many regions and eras claim rustic architecture as their own invention. They all have a

legitimate claim, as each has contributed in some way to what rustic design has become today. As this enduring and appealing style continues to evolve and diversify, all the traditional and modern interpretations will find a place under the umbrella of rustic architecture.

LEFT This New Hampshire lake house is based on the architecture of the Adirondack Great Camps of the early 1900s. It is laid out in the compound formation employed by William West Durant, the pioneer of this style. Peeled log columns and gable screens, brainstorm, and board and batten siding are all signatures of the Adirondack home.
Photograph by Cheryle St. Onge

BELOW RIGHT Architect Candace Tillotson-Miller's flawless rendition of Old West architecture is portrayed in this hallway at a ranch near Yellowstone Park.
© Mark Darley/Esto

Recently John Warren of Cashiers, North Carolina built the back cabin with a mill as a "play house." It is where the boys play cards and where John's bluegrass band practices. Architect Tim Greene designed the additions and outbuildings to be completely harmonious with the much revered original "picnic cabin".

PRIMITIVE BY NATURE:
THE BUILDING BLOCKS OF RUSTIC DESIGN

The natural world provides the raw materials for rustic architecture: stone, wood, bark, burl, and branch are the building blocks of this style. It is the cohesive manipulation of these elements that determines the success of a home. In the case of rustic architecture, the materials *are* the style. It's not so much the shape and form that identify a rustic home, but the choices that are made for building materials. The renaissance of the rustic style in the 1980s rekindled an interest in nature and its application in the building trades. This design style has enjoyed its own learning curve and progression regarding expertise in working with natural materials. Here is an illustrated look at how these materials are used in different parts of the country.

ABOVE A stonework still life in Tennessee fieldstone at The Canoe Club in Cashiers, North Carolina.

OPPOSITE This cabin near Big Sky Montana designed by Faure-Halvorsen Architects represents all of the best of the West. It is an eclectic blend of materials: reclaimed square-cut tamarack log, recycled red barnwood, native twig railings, stacked stone all off-set by a steel roof that has been allowed to rust. This winning combination successfully affects a timeworn "been here forever" character.

Photograph by gordongregoryphoto.com

STONE

S ince prehistoric times, man has used stone to define, worship, and protect that which he held most precious—his land. Stone formed by nature over millions of years is the oldest, most durable building product. Because it's expensive to quarry and more expensive to move from place to place, stone is the one building element that puts a regional tag on a home. One is able to identify a home in the Midsouth by Tennessee fieldstone, which has different characteristics from a New England granite.

This element can be as hard as granite (igneous), as soft as sandstone or limestone (sedimentary), or as varied as marble (metamorphic). It can be quarried or picked from a river bed or field. In its most humble form it is called "undressed," where it remains untouched by the tools of the trade. This is what is commonly used in rustic structures. Architects specify stone for the color, texture, pattern, and scale it can provide a project. It has a sense of permanence and the additional value of providing sound control, fire

At this Colorado home on the Eagle River, Telluride Gold stacked stone was used to step beyond its boundaries and become a natural outcropping.

resistance, and insulation against shifts in temperature. On exteriors stone is used for foundations, walkways, and landscaping, and inside for fireplaces, countertops, flooring, and some wall finishes.

The masons who work stone are a breed unto themselves. They risk physical wear from the weight of their medium. They are puzzle solvers who take pleasure in sifting through piles of rocks in search of the perfect piece to fill a particular gap. It takes real talent to put together a foundation wall or fireplace that is balanced and artful. There are two schools of thought on rustic masonry. One is to make the

stone appear dry laid with no mortar, for a natural, more primitive look that appears to be braced only by gravity. The other is to inset and accent the joints, making them baseball seams, wide, eye catching, and rustic. In either case composition is of paramount importance. Generally, the most successful rustic masonry displays larger rocks on the bottom gradating to smaller ones higher up, avoiding the monotony of a wall of uniformly sized stones.

Although it is the furthest thing from nature imaginable, cultured stone has come into favor as a substitute for rock. Often in a renovation, there is a lack of a proper support structure for such load bearing and the lighter weight, man-made stone is the only answer. Budgetary considerations may also make this an alternative. Additionally, many regions in the West have banned proper fire boxes and allow only gas-burning stoves, making cultured stone an acceptable option.

Hagrid's hut from the *Harry Potter* book series has been replicated at Camp Topridge as a playhouse for the children. It boasts an authentic straw roof created by a master thatcher brought to the site. Much of the elaborate stonework on the property was constructed by Lamphere Contracting.

CHAD SANBORN
Stonemason

This accomplished stone mason got his start while working on the embankments and culverts in New Hampshire's Franconia Notch, the former home of the Old Man of the Mountain (a tourist attraction portraying the stone profile of a man—in 2003 it slid down the mountain). His love of stone has brought him to a project on a New Hampshire lake, a home built almost entirely of granite inside and out and designed by Christopher P. Williams Architects. Sanborn and his team have been working stone here for fifteen months.

Each of the four fireplaces has a theme relating to Native Americans that is rendered in stone: canoe, arrow, and Indian chief among them. No drawings were required and all of the illustrations were worked out like a puzzle on the floor in each of the rooms. Much of the stone is reclaimed from older homes and the ever-present stone walls of this region. The weathered rock is highly marked with iron veins, moss, and lichen.

Chad Sanborn created mosaic images of an arrow and Indian in a canoe out of granite at this lakefront home in New Hampshire.

WOOD

Most of us look at trees for the shade they give or the neighbors they screen or as fuel for fire. The rustic woodworker sizes up a tree for its character and what it can become. The more duress a tree has been under, the more compelling to the wood artisan: burls, knots, and scars are beauty marks. These features distinguish one piece of wood from another and should be acknowledged in translating the raw materials into the structural or the decorative. Rustic woodworkers include the log workers who cope and notch the trees for log homes, the craftspeople who remove a slice from a tree leaving the wavy natural edge to be worked into a table or mantel, and the artists who carve bas-relief wildlife into a plank of wood to become a door panel or frieze.

A classic Elco electric launch (boat) sits in a highly rusticated new boathouse: a composition in serenity and cedar.

FINISHES

Experimentation with a variety of wood sidings both outside and in has made for interesting surfaces in the new rustic home. A Chinese menu of options can be successfully combined on an edifice to create appealing variations in color and texture.

Unpeeled log: Trees with bark on are harvested in the late fall and winter and used in true log construction or as decorative posts or trusses. This look is well known in the East and South. Cedar is employed in the Northeast as it is inherently resistant to bugs; spruce, white and red pine, and Ponderosa pine are also suitable. Poplar is favored in the South for its tight high-relief texture. As a rule, the designers in the West prefer the peeled log to the unpeeled.

Peeled log: This is the material used most often in log homes across the country. Bark is peeled from the tree in the spring when it's loose; a power washer can move the process along. The East has been heavily logged of its larger trees and yields log diameters in the 8" to 15" range. Larger timbers up to 36" are harvested in Montana, Wyoming, and Canada. In the East and Midwest red pine, cedar, and spruce are commonly used. In the West lodgepole pine, western red cedar, and Douglas fir are the logs of choice.

Half-log: Logs cut in half, usually with bark left on, applied as a veneer to a framed structure. Half-log siding is meant to have the semblance of a true log home.

Milled log siding: Logs that have been milled with a rounded side to look like uniform log siding.

Board and batten: Once relegated to sheathing for the tool shed, board and batten has taken its position as an attractive accompaniment to other rustic sidings in multiple material schemes. Very simply, it is board (often rough-sawn) that has a thin wood strip applied to cover the seam between two adjoining planks. Its cousin, board and channel, has a recessed channel strip. Both of these create a pleasant striping effect that works well with a contrasting siding of bark on log or brainstorm.

ABOVE A New Hampshire lake home takes the light approach to rustic. Small doses can be very effective; here a peeled gable and rafter detail does the trick.

OPPOSITE The simple concept of board and batten is elevated to an art form by artist Brad Corriveau. Battens were hand carved as sculpture in the form of oars, then affixed to the panels.

Shingle: Cedar shakes are the most rustic form of this barkless shingle and, because they are hand-split, they create an irregular cladding. Bark-on poplar shingles enjoy widespread popularity in the South and are surprisingly flat, stable and durable.

Brainstorm siding (aka Adirondack siding, feather board, hog pen, natural edge, waney edge): Boards that have the live edge or bark left on one edge. This is applied in the same manner as clapboard siding and creates an undulating, organic surface.

Slab siding: Slabs cut from the first pass through the planer, often with bark on. These boards are usually applied as decorative detail to framed structures.

LOGARHYTHM

Log construction specialists use various methods to interlock the timbers used in log construction. A regional history often plays a role in the method selected. The Swedish cope has a concave side for the tightest possible fit. The round log chink style uses round logs with a round notch, and a half- or full-dovetail corner; a chink gap is left between the logs to be finished with chinking. Broadaxe-hewn log style is easily identified by logs that are hewn square, with corners locked together and half- or full-dovetail corners.

An interior notched beam detail in the dovetail manner often used in the South.

ABOVE This North Carolina house features a combination of sidings: feather board, a variation on board and batten, and stone.

OPPOSITE TOP This close-up of a diamond-patterned door at Lean-To Camp illustrates not only the success of combining various sidings (board and batten run in perpendicular planes paired with bark on slab siding) in one facade but also the importance of color to the Adirondack camp.

OPPOSITE BOTTOM Copper and peeled cedar make a dramatic pairing for this railing.

PAUL STARK
Woodcarver

Paul Stark left art school in Portland, Oregon, to apprentice as a chain saw carver. He "performed" his craft of rendering wildlife from logs at street festivals and state fairs. Early in the 1990s, his work was featured in *Oregon Log Homes*. Since then he's been on the road eight months a year working on commissions all over the continent. Recently he completed "Sea of Life" a 10' x 5' panel for a Long Island hospital. His largest and most challenging job was the Dragon House at Topridge (below) where he worked under severe November weather conditions in the Adirondacks to complete this elaborate illustration.

Stark works mostly in pine, cedar, and walnut. He is fluent in both three-dimensional sculpture or bas-relief. What began as basic chain saw carving has evolved into fine art.

The Dragon House showcases marvelous and intricate woodcarving by the extremely talented Paul Stark.

RIGHT Bark panels secured by peeled cedar sheath a woodshed at a New Hampshire camp.

OPPOSITE Poplar shingles are ever present in the South as seen on this home at the Chatooga Club in Cashiers, North Carolina.

BARK

Originally used in Indian wigwams, the more current trend of enlisting bark as an architectural embellishment traces its origin to Camp Pine Knot in the Adirondacks. The first of the Great Camps, its creator used bark, twig, and log throughout, making it the springboard for the rustic design of over a century ago.

The heartier barks can be cut from the tree to be used for siding or stripped in sheets to be used as wallpaper or decoupage. Stripped bark is used more often in the East as the species there lend themselves to stripping: cedar, white birch, hemlock, and poplar. The bark is harvested when loose, generally in the spring and summer. Rings are cut around the tree and then an incision is cut lengthwise. The bark is easily peeled and treated with a solution (typically boric acid to kill bugs), pressed under weighted plywood to flatten curves, and then cut into shakes or left in thin sheets.

Bark is applied to exteriors as sheathing in the form of shakes, or in panels tacked in overlapping patchwork style. It requires minimal care except the occasional re-tacking of corners. In furniture, bark has many possibilities and experimentation in its use is an ongoing study. Birch bark seems to be the most popular for rustic furniture; both the white face side and reverse pinkish rind are used, sometimes in tandem. Bark sheets are easily attached by simply tacking and covering seams with half twigs or using an adhesive and securing the edges only with tacks. To achieve an aged look it is often varnished, which gives a protective coating that can be maintained with a vacuum.

ARTISAN AT WORK

LARRY HAWKINS
The Master of Birch Bark

This gentleman from the woods of Michigan got into the business of combining bark and furniture making after touring the Adirondacks. He procures his birch bark from local Native Americans and forages through the woods himself to find twigs that hold up to his standards. White birch is sought after for its bark; yellow birch, poplar, and red maple for the twigs he uses to secure it. He was influenced by the work of Ernest Stowe, a master of rustic cabinetry whose work with birch and twig over a century ago still impresses.

One of Hawkins' most challenging projects was a 2000-square-foot home covered in five van-loads of bark. As is the case with Hawkins and his comrades in the trade, he is constantly seeking new applications and combinations of materials to further his craft. He is the author of two how-to books on building mosaic twig furniture.

This patchwork bark dressing room was painstakingly pieced together. Hawkins used both the face and pinkish rind of white birch bark cut into 10-inch squares and tacked it down with 1-inch twigs that had been drying for a year. To protect the bark, two coats of urethane were applied.

Photograph courtesy Larry Hawkins

BURL, BRANCH, AND TWIG

Generally speaking, the finishing details of rustic architecture and furnishings are made from the portion of the tree that remains after the structure is erected. What is unusable for building works ideally for smaller pieces or furniture embellishments. As a rule of thumb, the further out on the limb, the more tedious the task becomes. Branches can be used in their entirety for railings or columns but when it gets down to the twig it becomes the work of a jeweler, precise and exacting. If the pieces aren't dried properly and applied with care, longevity is compromised. Rustic artistry is pure garnish taking the form of a burl kingpost, filigree twig gable screen, or branch towel bar. This is the lighthearted part of decoration, but can also be the kiss of death if restraint is not used.

Twigs are worked in an organic manner with all the curves and curly offshoots as part of the design, or they are cut into straight sections and applied as mosaic or parquetry. Often an artisan will choose many species to bring color variation to a piece. Burls are used in structural and furniture application and imagination dictates the treatment: left whole they can become a railing baluster or chair arm, split or sliced they make an exotic tabletop.

OPPOSITE A canoe shelter and deck at Camp Topridge in the Adirondacks features work by Jim Brush, who added the stream channel as a water feature. The craftsmen were encouraged to test their artistic and technical abilities, resulting in unexpected details at every turn.

ABOVE A peeled cedar railing wends its way into a foyer in an Adirondack home designed by Peter Pennoyer Architects and Ann Stillman O'Leary. The wall surface is a split barn timber with oakham chinking.
© Gary Hall Photography

DAN MACK
Twigmaster

Dan Mack from Warwick, New York has been experimenting with natural forms in twig since 1978. He is one of the most skilled craftsmen in his field. His work has achieved museum-quality status, characterized by strong and sculptural yet delicate and animated pieces and installations. Mack's work is featured in major galleries and museums, including the Smithsonian and the Museum of Fine Art in Boston. "I explore the forms, textures, and deformities of trees. I separate the trees from the forest, re-present and remember them. I want to keep the history of the tree present in the work and still reflect the hand and heart of the maker." His structural works and furniture pieces steal the show in any room (see page 191).

In his studio Dan Mack shapes nature into one of his remarkable memory chairs.
Photograph by David Horton

The Adirondack Rustics Gallery in Schroon Lake, New York showcases some of the finest rustic furniture from across the North Country. The work of Barry and Matthew Gregson is shown here. The chairs are a combination of root-y yellow birch, apple branch, and cherry burl. They have been sanded and contoured to the body for comfort. The coffee table is cut from a white birch burl and is supported by a lilac base.
Photograph courtesy Barry Gregson

IRON

In the hands of skilled artisans, iron becomes a decorative material. Man began working this metal as far back as 3500 BC, and ironwork enjoyed popularity until the Great Depression. Dormant as a livelihood until the recent revival of rustic homes, the products forged by the tools of the ironworker make an ideal choice for this architecture; the dull, black, rippled or scored surface plays well against wood tones.

Iron is formed in two ways: it can be cast (molten iron is poured into prepared sand molds) or it can be wrought (globules or rods are heated over a furnace and forged into shape with a hammer on an anvil.) Wrought iron has become an essential ingredient of the rustic home. Markings acquired in the forging process grant character and perfection is deemed undesirable. Iron accents can be seen in hinges, railings, gates, drapery hardware, lighting, and fireplace tools. Often referred to as the common man's metal, it has enhanced many of the great rustic buildings of recent times.

ABOVE A lifelike bronze bear and pine tree lantern cast by Peter Fillerup.
Photograph by Matt Turley Photographer

RIGHT Craftsmanship is of paramount importance at Topridge, even down to the outdoor railings. Here cast claws anchor the branch-like aluminum rails along the network of pathways that connect the many buildings on the compound.

CHRISTOPHER THOMSON
Metal Magician

On the frontage road outside of Santa Fe sits the Christopher Thomson Ironworks. He creates forged steel lamps, candlesticks, lighting, fireplace tools, and furniture. Thomson began his career 20 years ago by training in clay as a medium, working with a master potter. "Clay moves in ways similar to hot steel, but is quicker to work with. The repetition and sheer volume of work I was able to make as a production potter helped me train my eye and to develop an aesthetic which applies to my forged steel work." His designs are hand-forged in steel; he and his five assistants hammer, stretch, and bend the red-hot steel into the desired forms. Pieces are shaped, sized, welded, buffed, and straightened; each item is hand finished with one of four custom finishes then stamped with his logo. Thomson's pieces have a spare sculptural quality that sets them apart from others in the field (see examples on pages 199 and 200.)

Hammer and anvil form molten iron into a light fixture at the hands of Christopher Thomson.
Photograph courtesy Christopher Thomson Ironworks

ABOVE One of the amazing light fixtures forged by Chicken Coop Forge in the Adirondacks.
Photograph courtesy Chicken Coop Forge

OPPOSITE In New Hampshire, architect Deirdre Sheerr-Gross has reached a compromise between the tradition of separate-use rooms and the open great room concept by using simple architectural elements to define areas without confining the space. The substantial granite fireplace becomes the screen between the great room and dining area. Additional volume is borrowed visually from adjacent areas with each room benefiting from the barter of space.

THE REGIONAL ROOTS OF RUSTIC

Although the lines are getting blurry, there are certain characteristics that identify rustic architecture from one region to the next. Much of it has to do with indigenous materials, weather conditions, and architects who advance their particular design ethic. The simple lay of the land often dictates the scale and proportion of a home—the majestic mountain homes of the West require an appropriately scaled log that would overwhelm a home in Wisconsin. Context is a word spoken in unison by architects across the country. In the regions examined, it seemed that the design teams take one of two approaches: capture the essence of historic rustic homes in the area and reinterpret them, or distill the information into a hybrid style that becomes the architect's signature. Once they have put their imprimatur on the landscape and have proliferated their design ethic, it becomes the look for that geographical region.

Looking at the features and materials that distinguish rustic design from one area of the country to another, it's interesting to note that some materials are named one thing in one region and something else in a different area—for instance the Adirondack term "brainstorm siding" is known as "feather board" in the South, "live edge" board in New England, and "waney edge" in other regions. (All these terms refer to the boards cut in planks with a natural edge remaining.) The vernacular hasn't caught up to the trade.

THE NORTHEAST

In the Northeast one would think that the neighboring states of New York, Vermont, and New Hampshire would share a common thread or rustic ideology. This is not the case; there isn't even a proper road that runs east to west, much less an exchange of ideas. Architects and interior designers are acting autonomously here, unaware of their impact on the genre as a whole.

The Adirondack style relies heavily on the past, using the Great Camps as a model for new interpretations. The look relies on deep overhangs, steep roof pitches, hipped roofs, and connecting walkways. The sidings used in the North Country are varied and interesting: bark-on spruce, hemlock, and cedar; peeled log, slab siding, and brainstorm. The birch tree and its bark are used more in the Adirondacks than anywhere—trunk, limb, branch, and twig are used here. The stunning white sheathing is commonly seen as decoration on exteriors and interiors and is used exuberantly on furniture. The railings of the Adirondacks are the looms upon which twig workers weave their magic; they tend to be more organic and imaginative than their counterparts across the country.

Interiors are decidedly dark, due in part to the deep overhangs, heavily wooded settings, and association with old camps of the late Victorian era. Deep rich colors such as Navajo reds and forest greens are used enthusiastically to battle grey light and chronic weather conditions. There is an abundance of "stuff" in the typical Adirondack home. It is safe to say that clutter reigns supreme in the North Country.

This Adirondack rustic style has found its way to every region in the country; it is the most animated of all of the rustic styles and there is a rich library of inspiration to draw from.

Vermont proffers a less severe, lighter version of rustic. Wood is left its natural pale color, logs are peeled, walls are painted white or off-white. There is an absence of the academic need to be historically correct because there is no real history of rustic in the land of the saltbox and farmhouse. Homes in this region are more sparsely furnished than their Adirondack cousins. There is a bare minimum of floor covering, furniture, and a notable lack of gewgaws and artifacts.

The lake and mountain homes of New Hampshire's White Mountains were traditionally rendered in the shingle style of architecture made popular at the turn of the last century. This style was familiarized by the seaside vacation homes of New England and was comfortably adapted to inland and mountain homes. There are rustic homes in this region but they tend to be based on traditional shingle-style format with log accents.

BELOW This great room at a home on Lake Placid represents new camp decor conveyed through rough-hewn board-and-batten walls, a cultured stone fireplace, and vibrantly colored furnishings. Designed by Ann Stillman O'Leary.
© Gary Hall Photography

The shingle-style home is known for additions and continuous, rambling architecture. The genre originated with a legitimate need for more space and the wish to remain inside while moving from one end of the house to the other.

New Hampshire shingle-style mountain homes are characterized by the cedar shingles, granite foundations and masonry, and Douglas fir bead board interiors. Occasionally a peeled log is worked in. More recently, architects and builders have foraged the woods and brought more of the natural world into these homes, coming closer to an Adirondack or Vermont rendition of rustic.

Oddly, the rustic architecture and design sensibility of central Maine is closer in kinship to the Adirondack camp model than to neighboring New Hampshire or Vermont. They even refer to their homes as camps and decorate them in the same manner as their New York counterparts.

ABOVE An outbuilding at Camp Topridge in the Adirondacks illustrates the sculptural possibilities of cedar, often used in this region.

THE SOUTH

The mountain homes of the South enlist grayish-greenish exterior logs or timber as an element in many structures. Square logs (broadaxe hewn) predominate and are dressed with wide swaths of chinking. The bark of the poplar tree is robust and scabby, making fabulous bark shingles for inside and out. Locust railings are de rigueur; the laurel balusters are usually vertical and of a consistent diameter, differentiating them from the cedar railings of the Northeast. Other identifiable features are the use of feather board, gold rectangular Tennessee fieldstone, metal roofs, and the ever-present porch.

In the Confederacy the furnishings are decidedly much more formal than those in the Northeast or Midwest. This is parlor country. Lush appointments amidst a rustic setting bedeck proper dining rooms, sitting rooms, and libraries. Draperies, not curtains, dress windows, European antiques keep company with rustic accessories in what is altogether a more deliberate, styled look.

THE MIDWEST

In the Midwest, log construction is the most common permutation of rustic. The regional vernacular is vaguely Swedish in feel, especially in Minnesota. New construction yields to

BELOW An outbuilding at a home in Cashiers, North Carolina designed by architect Tim Greene portrays the rustic of the South in the square-cut timber (adze hewn) siding and broken pitch metal roof common in this region.

This property, built in 1912 in Oregon City, Oregon is one of the oldest and largest log home retreats listed on the National Historic Register that is used as a single-family retreat. Scandinavian craftsmen working in the Adirondack rustic style oversaw the construction of the home, which has since been restored. It features a great room measuring over 1000 square feet with a 22-foot-high lodgepole ceiling, split-log stairs, and two interior balconies.

Photograph by Roger Wade

convention in this neck of the woods. There are a number of log home companies in the Midwest known for superior quality and engineering. They will work with an architect's plan or design a custom home for the client. The homes are put together at the manufacturers to insure proper fit. The logs are numbered and disassembled then shipped to a job site for reassembly. Generally the log homes in this region are unstained, creating pale bright interiors, though some of the older homes adopted a darker stain as an ode to the Adirondack Great Camp. Furnishings tend to be practical and comfortable and have little regional flavor.

THE NORTHWEST

It's all about logs here—Douglas fir and western red cedar specifically. There is a rich history of rustic architecture in the Northwest that dates back to the gold rush era which was defined during the early 1900s by the structures of the National Park Service, specifically Crater Lake Lodge, and, the marvel in log: the Timberline Lodge. Today the log homes being built in the Northwest generally bow to tradition with a few notable exceptions that have transformed log into unexpected modernistic dwellings that have garnered national press.

THE WEST

In the West, rustic architecture falls into one of three categories: Old West, resort architecture, and New West. The rustic homes and ranches there play to the romanticism of the Old West, conjuring up visions of pioneering, the gold rush, Wild Bill Cody, and dude ranches (which became popular during WW I when Europe was designated off limits). The big sky and cowboy country spirit is captured in these homes. The most successful of these are neither ostentatious nor do they trivialize the style. Because restraint is the order of the day, these structures are straightforward and unadorned, taking the form of log cabins showing heavily marked timbers, rusted tin roofs, barn board, and plenty of regional stone (many permutations of sandstone are readily available).

The resort architecture of the West is a crossbreed of the idyllic ranches associated with pioneering and efficient contemporized vacation homes—with limited historic ties but a deference to the landscape and native materials.

The New West announces itself through condensed forms hinting at the essence of a structure, through the synthesis of glass, metal, timber, and stone. This modern expression of rustic is beginning to gain in popularity and is being celebrated in regional and national shelter publications, which will aid in promoting the look. These dynamic homes are intended to promote an interactive experience between man and his surroundings.

The three faces of Western rustic design have a shared aesthetic when it comes to the interiors: a neutral palette featuring wood, brown stone, off-white integral plaster walls, and the counterplay of leather and chenille against a canvas of smooth and coarse variations on an earthy theme.

A Lake Tahoe cabin designed by architect Greg Faulkner and interior designer Tina Vallone pays homage to the old bungalows of the region. It brings the outside in with reclaimed exterior siding taken from a local mill.

Photograph by Dino Tonn Photography

LEFT This magnificent home sits slope-side at a ski resort in the Rockies. Architect Douglas M. DeChant has skillfully enunciated his version of new rustic in this modern-day Alpine lodge that takes detail and craftsmanship to a new level.

BELOW Wildwood, designed by the progressive firm CCY Architects, is the embodiment of New West architecture. Although the forms are abstract, the siting and material choices tie it to the land, making it analogous to its environs.

© Robert Millman Photography

The new boathouse at Camp Topridge in the Adirondacks.

A PORTFOLIO OF RUSTIC HOMES:

30 OF THE BEST RUSTIC DESIGNS IN NORTH AMERICA

A coast-to-coast house tour takes a look at what is current in regional rustic architecture. This armchair expedition journeys from the shingle-style rustic of New Hampshire to the Cracker-inspired homes of the Carolinas to the log structures of Minnesota and Canada. Traveling westward, we visit contemporary resort architecture and homesteads with historic ties in Colorado, Montana, and California. Running the spectrum from a 600-square-foot cabin to a 10,000-square-foot futuristic stone-and-steel spaceship, the rustic style is being adopted and adapted across the continent. This is what is happening and where it's going.

In the manner of the older camps of these lakes the architecture rambles, a two-and-a-half story glass filled central structure is the anchor for the main house with two wings splayed out from the axis. Varied rooflines including cross-gables, shed dormers, and polygons break up the mass of the camp, and aided by the airy twig gable screens, impart a lightness to the camp. The web-like gable screens were inspired by those seen in the Great Camps of the Adirondacks.

Photograph by Cheryle St. Onge

IN THE GREAT TRADITION

The Great Camps of the Adirondacks, the structures of the National Park Service, and the grand mountain vacation homes of the post-industrial revolution were all built when the term "leisure time" was newly coined. They have become the models for a new generation of homebuilders trying to capture a slice of the past. The homes in this section draw from tradition and take their cues from these forebears. The legacy continues, paying homage to the past through composition, the use of conventional materials, and long-established methods of construction.

NEW ENGLAND NATURAL
NEW HAMPSHIRE

ARCHITECT: CHRISTOPHER P. WILLIAMS ARCHITECTS
BUILDER: WHITEHOUSE CONSTRUCTION
INTERIOR DESIGN: CLARK PLANNING AND DESIGN, MARY CLARK CONLEY

For over a century, lake-house architecture in New Hampshire was relegated to shingle style and clapboard houses. Historically there were few truly rustic structures in these parts, the New England model being simpler and less exuberant than their showy New York counterparts in the Adirondacks. Architect Chris Williams has recast the die and has become the eminence grise of natural architecture in this region. He is well-versed in the building vernacular of these lakes; his family has summered here since 1870.

In the spirit of cross-pollination this exceptional lakefront compound of three buildings and outbuildings heavily references the Adirondack Great Camps built over a century ago, while maintaining a Yankee dignity appropriate for the lake it's on. A project of this magnitude and complexity had not been attempted in this region for over a hundred years. There is a learning curve to working in unprocessed materials; it is by definition an inexact science. Woodworkers must deal with the caprice of Mother Nature—there are few 90-degree angles, and miter boxes are useless in this trade; scribing and coping are essential skills. The strategy was to begin with the boathouse, segue to the guesthouse, and finish with the main house, with the understanding that, along the way, a degree of precision would be perfected by the architect, builder, and interior designer who were experimenting with form, function, and nature.

This compound is wedded to its site; the buildings all relate to each other and collectively they connect to the land. The basic structural forms are executed in the spirit of the older camps on this lake where roof pitches at 10 over 12 are quintessential New Hampshire-lakes region. It is the choice of material, embellishments, and details that make this home rustic. Wavy-edge siding (aka brainstorm) was selected for the body of the buildings, tongue-and-groove paneling and cedar shingles were introduced to play up texture. Peeled log gable screens and flared-foot tree columns make these buildings one with their environment. The structures are understated but the degree of detail is strong and unfolds as one enters each space.

The level of craftsmanship is unparalleled in the main house; the artisans were given license to be imaginative and the results exceeded expectations. There are hidden compartments, camouflaged light fixtures, artwork integrated into the structure, and an element of surprise and humor in every room.

A certain synergy is attained when the home and furnishings are fully conceived while still on the drawing board (this is being termed site-specific today). To create harmony, interior designer Mary Clark Conley had the challenge of designing site-specific furniture tailored to this house and this owner. The dining table was configured into six individual square tables that could be put together in any formation to seat four or twenty-four. A server was calculated to sit at the exact height of a row of window muntins so as not to disturb a line of vision.

A curvaceous tree that had grown over a boulder was brought intact to the job site by log worker Mark Smith; the crew deemed it ideal for the stair rail. To install the freeform piece it was necessary to create a footing. A hole was cut in the floor framing, an extra pillar added in the basement, the boulder set into concrete, and the newel post/branch attached as if the forest floor had grown into the foyer.

Three types of trees are represented in the twig "dentil" border that wraps the main level at the transom height and leads to the dining room. The banding emulates books on a shelf and was applied to break up the vertical planes of the space.

ABOVE The scale of this room needed to be reined in and made more intimate; Williams brought the upper level in like the clerestory of a church to control the air space. The interior logs are spruce harvested from northern Maine. Log worker Mark Smith removed the bark with a pressure washer, leaving a smooth, sinuous hand. New Hampshire has been dubbed "the granite state" and there is no limit to the spectrum of surface or coloration of this stone. The fireplace stone is aged granite quarry remnants that are rife with texture and character. The floors throughout are of antique heart pine and the woodwork is pine. As a relief from the wood (and to visually lighten the space), the architect wrapped the interior with a band of drywall that was troweled with plaster.

The fireplace surround is of special interest, composed of replica arts and crafts tiles from California that were custom-colored by the architect to coordinate with the rugs.

RIGHT A grand entryway to a grand camp. This intricate door was embellished in twig mosaic and illuminated by a leaded glass window created by the Lyn Hovey Studios.

OPPOSITE All of the rustic details in the house are integral to the structure. The stone arch became the solution to a design dilemma: two fireplace flues needed to converge at the core of the camp. This confluence became a handsome design element in the guest wing.

LEFT A study in glass. This elegant window was a collaborative effort between Alice Johnson of the Lyn Hovey Studios and Chris Williams. The owner requested that leitmotifs from nature be carried through the guest-house and main house. In the guest house, the theme is flora and the main house, fauna.

BOTTOM LEFT Flared white-cedar log posts on the porch form a root colonnade.

BOTTOM RIGHT An exciting combination of light and animal imagery merges in this elaborate copper chandelier that hangs in the entry. It was made by artisan Dennis Sparling and is one of the many custom pieces he created for the camp.

OLD TAHOE FOLK ART LIVING
CALIFORNIA

ARCHITECT: FAULKNER ARCHITECTS—GREG FAULKNER, AIA, PRINCIPAL ARCHITECT
BUILDER: SITECRAFT CONSTRUCTION INTERIOR DESIGN: VALLONE DESIGN, INC.—DONNA VALLONE AND CAROLINE DeCESARE

This inventive California home is part cabin, part barn, part bungalow, and all Old Tahoe. Perched on a wooded hillside overlooking the Martis Creek meadow, the home won the 2005 Tahoe Quarterly Mountain Home Award in the category of "Unique Expression." The exterior is intentionally understated while the interior is funky cabin-cum-art gallery. It reflects the spirit of Old Tahoe homes in engaging material choices and variation of forms accentuated by the cantilevered rooflines. Designed as a stage set for a collection of folk art, it has become, in itself, an expression of Tahoe style. "We wanted the house to be modest," says architect Greg Faulkner, "very anti-iconographic and with a lot of familiar Old Tahoe forms added together." It is in fact a collage of small recognizable indigenous shapes—cabins, porches, shed additions, flat roofs, gables, and exposed rafter tails that tell the story of this California mountain town.

Where possible, local materials were used thoughtfully to promote the historic and regional personality of the home. The look is idiosyncratic but ultimately very appealing and as honest as the art it showcases. Cobblestones reclaimed from a salami factory find a place next to salvaged Douglas fir floorboards. Metal has been woven into the fabric of the home where possible, but stone was used sparingly (only as retaining walls) because Old Tahoe houses didn't use stone veneer. There is a dose of outside/in in this house; exterior siding has been used for paneling, rafter tails end inside rather than out, riveted metal accents are used on both exteriors and interiors—the concept is well executed and cohesive. On the interior, color has been used with abandon; the intensity plays well against the dark oiled wood of the home and sets off the selectively placed treasures.

OPPOSITE The stacked rooflines are an ode to Old Tahoe, creating positive and negative space, allowing nature to peek through. Corten roofing has rusted to a perfect hue; this material has a protective coating to prevent it from rusting through—it is a durable choice. Reclaimed redwood siding from a local barn still displays the stamps from the Hobart Mills, a defunct lumber company from nearby Truckee.

Photograph by Greg Faulkner

ABOVE Heavy timbers, rustic iron accents, and overtones of National Park structures commingled with Arts and Crafts bungalow style to connect this home to the buildings of Old Tahoe.

Photograph by Greg Faulkner

LEFT The unusual and well-researched selection of materials becomes a canvas for the lively color in this kitchen, setting off the folk art and furnishings. Planes are broken up by altering finishes, a wall of long-leaf heart pine (from a tobacco drying barn in Kentucky) is interrupted by a painted olive or ochre wall with oiled wood wainscot. The owners' request for whimsy was met with the designer's specification for a checkerboard backsplash.
Photograph by Dino Tonn Photography

OPPOSITE The inspiration for the color scheme for this house came from a knit sock the owner brought to the first design meeting announcing, "I love these colors and want this palette for my new house." Designers Donna Vallone and Caroline DeCesare gladly acquiesced and delivered a plan that was colorful, eclectic, folk-arty, and fun. Local granite was used to form the fireplace, which acts as a divider between the great room and the media room.
Photograph by Dino Tonn Photography

BELOW LEFT The pattern of ceiling rafters suspended at different angles creates a sculptural grid above the living space. Cut nails were used rather than nail guns to maintain historic integrity. The textural banquette is covered in woven leather and serves as an informal dining area, while the adjacent sitting area has become a place to watch sports events with four televisions embedded into the custom cabinetry. A sliding glass and pine barn door separates office space from the media area.
Photograph by Dino Tonn Photography

ADIRONDACK METAMORPHOSIS
NEW YORK

ARCHITECT: **NILS EDWARD LUDEROWSKI, AIA** BUILDER: **REDWING CONSTRUCTION, DAN NARDIELLO**

This is a story of metamorphosis: how an unprepossessing structure, in the form of a one-story shed, was transformed into an original and stunning camp compound. The property on Upper Saranac Lake in the Adirondack Mountains sits on a canoe carry road—a clearing used for boat portage. The owners purchased the land with its modest shelter in 1999 and set about finding an architect who could articulate their vision.

A well-informed client is a dream for an architect, and these owners came armed with 600 photos of Craftsman and shingle-style homes and design features that appealed to them. Luderowski distilled this information into a design that was representative of the rich culture of this lake. Rather than follow one particular design ethic, he fused multiple elements into a winning composition. In his words he "referred to all that had been done in rustic architecture from 1880 to 1940 and let it congeal in my head." There are overtones of shingle style as well as allusions to the architecture of Japan and Norway, styles often referenced in Adirondack camps of that time period.

To test the merit of Luderowski's design, the owners began by building "Catchall" a garage/workshop/office. It was a simple structure with a prominent gable that became the "overcoat" for the building. From there they moved on to "May as Well" ("If we put on the porch we may as well add the outdoor shower. And if. . .), and in short order Birch Point became a compound by happenstance.

When it came to the main house the team was technically unable to elaborate on the existing shed-like shelter, so Luderowski seized the opportunity to do something dramatic and draped it with another edifice, leaving the entire original "coop" intact. By manipulating form and material he was able to model the camp into a compelling structure. The porches could have been set square to the house but instead were turned and expressed as boat-like figures, a shape alien but harmonious to the gable and shed. A shower tower added at the last moment anchors the road side of the camp. The skirting detail is a signature of Luderowski's, continuing the silhouette of the structure and grounding it; he likens the feature to cuffs on a pair of pants.

Shingles were applied with caprice in a variety of sizes and shapes. The dictate was "throw in a paddle shake every now and then." Three colors were used in chorus on the exterior: black, dark brown, and green with red used occasionally to tweak the scheme. The triad was expected to cast a spectrum of countless colors at any given time depending upon light and shadow.

The handsome interiors reflect the architect's inclination for contemporary finishes and the owners' Great Camp sensibility. Camps of the North Country are traditionally dark, so the wood was kept natural—oiled, not stained—and the furnishings provide the depth of color and texture needed to achieve the updated rustic look.

OPPOSITE Camp Birch Point sits on a lakeside slope thick with trees and brush, it is virtually impossible to capture on camera. This is the architect's rendition of the very asymmetrical main house that grew from a shanty.
Drawing courtesy Nils E. Luderowski

ABOVE "Catchall", the multiple-use building on the grounds illustrates the Scandinavian influence in the eyebrow roofline and angled piers. Exaggerated contours on this simple structure lend a jocular personality. The blackish-brown stain and red trim are reminiscent of the palette used at Santanoni, one of the original Great Camps of the Adirondacks.

ABOVE Striving for "old camp" in the great room, the team specified materials that would have been used a century ago: Douglas fir vertical grain siding, pine flooring, tin ceilings. The architect is a modernist at heart and introduced a Rama, which is a Japanese element known as a frieze in the west. The twig banding runs the perimeter of the room above the door frames and divides the vertical space, controlling the scale and humanizing proportion in a room of this size. The home is filled with campy treasures amassed before the house was conceived, the coffee table is a 9' antique bobsled, lamps were fashioned from old stills, andirons are circa 1915 from Big Wolf Lake—all set amidst the stage set of Old Hickory furniture.

OPPOSITE This lakeside porch hangs in the treetops. The chaise is actually a cure bed intended for tuberculosis patients who came to these mountains to reclaim their health. The cure cottage traditionally featured multiple porches for year-round use and was conceived by Dr. E.L. Trudeau who built them throughout the Saranac Lake region of the Adirondacks.

ABOVE Luderowski took advantage of the site when positioning the master bedroom. The room has windows on all four walls and reaps the benefit of sunlight throughout the day. The architect is a devotee of the built-in, a Scandinavian conceit; the bed/storage unit he designed hugs the floor and leaves the impression of a captain's quarters on a ship. The twig cobwebs woven between two trees are a nod to the more conventional definition of rustic. The bark and twig work throughout was executed by local craftsman Bill Beatrice. Beyond this stand of trees, in a sunken area, is the owner's office.

OPPOSITE TOP The entry to camp is an Adirondack time warp owing to the deep brown backgrounds, rustic antiques, and amusing and unexpected fish scale application of birch bark ceiling shingles, an oft repeated motif on this project.

LEFT To convey daylight (or the illusion of it) to the center of the house Luderowski designed a substantial window to pour light onto the oversized stairway. The stairwell is the spiritual core of this camp, it is meant to encapsulate architecture within architecture and features a contemporary rustic railing with Japanese overtones. Crowned by maple burls the newell posts mimic the pylons on the exterior of the house and are skinned in a fish-scale pattern. The gothic iron bat pendant is an exclamation point in the open airspace and marks the transition of high to low. All of the new ironwork at the camp was forged by Eric Reece.

SMOKY MOUNTAIN MAGIC

NORTH CAROLINA

ARCHITECTS: **ORIGINAL HOME: HAL AINSWORTH AND WINTON NOAH** RENOVATION ARCHITECT: **GREENE AND ASSOCIATES, TIM GREENE**
BUILDER: **TOP NOTCH LOG COMPANY** RENOVATION: **JOHN LUPOLI** INTERIOR DESIGN: **LYNN MONDAY**

Here the mission for the architect and interior designer was to take a cabin that had been outfitted top to bottom in lively, high-cabin decor and subdue it with a more elegant, European lodge look. The home was originally designed and owned by the talented Atlanta design duo, Hal Ainsworth and Winton Noah, and was a well-documented example of their work—in this case a log cabin with a regional personality. Many of the finishes and some of the furniture remain in place. The new owners elected to renovate, seeking something more stately—a style that could be termed Carolina High Rustic.

The renovation team of Tim Greene and Lynn Monday rearranged the floor plan in a set of Rubik's Cube moves that involved transforming a porch into the dining room, the dining room into a drawing room, heightening the doors, and adding a screened porch, a wine cellar, and an entire guest wing. They landed at the finish line with a very polished southern version of mountain rustic. This home has a presence that speaks of the rustic tradition of the Smoky Mountains; square-cut log and stone commingled with board and batten, a long running porch sporting a row of rocking chairs, muted wood tones, and dusty paint colors, all against a backdrop of split rail fences, rhododendrons, and oak trees. You know you are in the heart of the Carolinas when you see this house that sits high on Big Sheepcliff Mountain overlooking a spectacular valley below.

This home is easily identified as a Carolina Mountain home. The roof pitch, sitting porch, square-hewn log poplar shingle, and Tennessee fieldstone foundation are telltale signs.

ABOVE Lynn Monday showed a reverence for tradition in furnishing the great room. The center-piece is a 100-year-old, museum-quality Agra rug. She imported the leather sofa from England and worked in two bespoke cabinets from France that had been left by the origi-nal owner. These European antiques have been introduced to their American cousins: locally made twig mirrors, faux fur tuffets, and assorted rustic accessories. The original walls remain— the highly textured poplar with bark-on shakes form an irregular pattern that plays well against the static wide and bright stripes produced by the chinking. Floors through-out the house are black walnut with clear stain— providing a great range of color.

RIGHT The library of a Southern gentleman. Generally, the interior décor of the Southern rustic home is far more polished than its counter-parts across the country. It is a fancy version of rustic with European allu-sions that capture the imagination here. In this richly appointed office twig marquetry cabinets flank a Black Forest clock.

OPPOSITE In the newly added guest quarters, this sumptuous suite is paneled in cherry and outfitted like the Ritz by designer Lynn Monday. Faux fur throws and heavily carved French library cabinets complete the European lodge look.

ABOVE LEFT This playful guest room has an unexpected piece of wall décor, a canoe hung cleverly in the rafters.

ABOVE RIGHT The original dining room was converted into this drawing room that provides a quiet setting for a glass of port by the fire.

HIGH PEAKS PERCH

NEW YORK

ARCHITECT: **Robert Bradbury** BUILDER: **Biesmeyer's Adirondack Building and Contracting, Inc., Bob Biesmeyer**
INTERIOR DESIGN: **Barbara Hart Interior Design, Barbara Hart and Pamela Kostmayer**

This mountaintop aerie sits on the ledges where the native black bears live in the High Peaks region of the Adirondacks, hence the name it was given: Bear Ledges. In an age of fear and terrorism this camp was intended to be a safe haven for four generations of a family that has been coming to this area for decades.

The site was extraordinarily challenging, as the drop-off is precipitous. The structure is built in to the granite ridge of Baxter Mountain, parts of which peek out from the skirting and foundation of the finished home. When pouring the foundation for the house every form had to be scribed to conform to the ledge. The genesis for the design were the monasteries of Lhasa, Tibet, expressed in gabled structures supported by massive tapered masonry bases. These twin stone masses flank the converging stairways. Because of the narrow ridge, the only feasible floor plan included a linear series of rooms—coincidentally this provided splendid vistas from every space. The placement and selection of window type was key to alleviating some weight from the exterior of the structure and bringing the desired light inside. The archi-

tect chose the Frank Lloyd Wright series from Marvin Windows for the job.

To reduce the visibility of the house from the mountains and valley spread out below, the exterior was finished in bark-on red pine slab siding, local stone, and a baked-enamel green metal roof. Allie Pelletier, well-known in the Adirondacks for his nimble masonry, did the majority of the stonework on the facade. The steps and walkways are all constructed of unpolished Adirondack green granite that has been scored and broken, no buffing or polishing allowed. As a transition to the bark siding a granite cap was added to the foundation level.

On the inside, impressive trusswork defines the main space of this camp. The logs were shipped whole from Montana and are made of peeled Douglas fir measuring up to 22" in diameter. The interior is bright and airy, unusual for this neck of the woods. Walls and logwork have been left unstained but were sealed to maintain a pale color. In the tradition of the Great Camp, decorative collections are a travelogue of the owners' journeys.

RIGHT The imposing edifice is exaggerated by the angle from which it is seen at the entry. At the closest point to the house the driveway is still some 30 feet below the main floor. The perspective distorts the structure and reinforces the grandeur of the camp.

OPPOSITE The great room is energized by a brightly colored Tibetan rug and vibrant fabric covered upholstered pieces. This well-traveled family proudly exhibits bridal Bribe Boxes from Ziachang, China, glass mosaic deer from the Huichol Indians in Mexico, and a Zulu beaded fertility goddess hat in the same arena as an Adirondack snakeskin box.

RIGHT The owner played an integral role in fleshing out the details of the camp. She designed the yellow birch railing that brings the visitor up to the main floor of the house. A dumbwaiter was installed to transport provisions to the kitchen and great room level. The large basket is part of the owners' collection. It is circa 1850 Navajo from Santa Fe and won first prize in a national basket competition. The Navajo rugs are authentic.

OPPOSITE TOP Treetops provide the scenery for the cantilevered porch. The flooring is mahogany, and the table is believed to be from the veteran rustic furniture maker Gib Jaques.

OPPOSITE BOTTOM LEFT The Pasha Pit, as it is fondly called, offers an exotic reading nook for grandkids and is itself a story of globetrotting. The quilt on the left is a gift from a woman's quilting guild in Cape Town, South Africa, and the wall hanging on the right is a beaded tapestry from Zanzibar. The intricate carved screens are Chinese and made from camphor wood.

OPPOSITE BOTTOM RIGHT Mike Trivieri designed and carved all of the bas-relief panels depicting wildlife. This one is a series in the entryway that tells the story of the terrapin. It is carved in butternut with Douglas fir trim.

HOME ON THE RANGE
MONTANA

ARCHITECT: **CTM Architects, Candace Tillotson-Miller, AIA**
BUILDER: **Yellowstone Traditions, Harry Howard** INTERIOR DESIGNERS: **Charles Gandy and Bill Peace**

A spectacular "big country" setting was the location selected for Sawtooth Mountain Ranch. This property at the rim of Yellowstone National Park in Montana is the habitat for elk herds, grizzly bear, and loads of wildlife. This is cowboy country. The ranch was an historic homestead built in the late 1800s when this magnificent park was begun and came with a trapper's cabin and barn. The design team chanelled the spirits of these pioneer dwellings to form the main house.

Architect Candace Tillotson-Miller and builder Harry Howard have a history together and are accomplished in executing the best of the Old West. Known for their sensitive application of indigenous and reclaimed materials, the net result is always traditional, restrained, and elegantly rustic. Tillotson-Miller relies on certain tenets of architecture to attain the proper balance: massing (simple yet elegant forms), rhythm (subtle, not tricked out), and texture achieved through the use of native and aged materials. It is a look that is timeless in appeal. The ranch conjures up images of homesteaders, German and Swedish pioneers of the Old West, and is a direct reference to the cabins they built from the materials at hand in this region.

From the Appalachian Mountains, the owner tracked down two barns built in the late 1800s that were made from square-hewn logs, typical of that region. These became the springboard for the design of the ranch. As was characteristic of these structures, the logs are a mix of oak, chestnut, poplar, and pine (whatever the land would yield) and they were assembled in no particular sequence. The construction mode of choice is 2 x 6 framed walls clad with this historic log veneer. It is an architectural sleight of hand that allows for larger windows and structural stability in this seismic zone. One of the barns was "rebuilt" as the main body of the house and the other as the master suite. The onus was on the contractor to find like-minded materials for the rest of the project to harmonize with these buildings.

The alluring interiors mirror the exteriors in finishes: the same log beams are sawn and applied to the walls in irregular spacing, the chinking runs between 1" and 5" thick. (Western chinking used to be made of chicken wire, straw, and dung.) Douglas fir is the preferred local wood and was used in tandem with reclaimed oak for flooring. Wax provides an added layer of age to the wood surfaces; the aural experience promotes the western mystique.

Subdued and unselfconscious, the interiors rely on texture and variation on an earthtone color scheme to achieve a quiet elegance. Burlap draperies, oiled leather seating, hand-planed wood, and hammered iron create quiet ambience in this sepia tone still life.

OPPOSITE The ghosts of two Appalachian barns are fully integrated into the ranch house on this breathtaking parcel on the old frontier. The building is a testament to the honesty of the pioneer homesteads of the 1800s. "Simple forms" and "no pretenses" are the catchphrases—the front stoop and twin dormers the only concession to architectural embellishment. Every board and piece of stone in this house has been hand picked for its veracity and then reworked on site. As Harry Howard of Yellowstone Traditions states, "This is a soulful house."

Photograph by gordongregoryphoto.com

ABOVE Tillotson-Miller strives to make spaces comfortable and intimate, not overwhelming. Getting the essence of a room to appear simple is a lesson in restraint. The color palette throughout the ranch is intentionally quiet, allowing the landscape to speak and the occupants to bring in pieces with personality. Harlowton Stone was stacked with recessed grout to appear dry laid and forms the fireplace. This sandstone litters the prairies of Montana and because it is exposed comes naturally weathered with lichen and moss as a bonus.

© Mark Darley/Esto

RIGHT A cottage-style Eastlake bed is the main attraction in the guest room. Wide swaths of chinking provide a strong horizontal stripe as a backdrop to the carefully edited ornaments telling the story of western homestead living: pelts, creels, and animal skulls.
© Mark Darley/Esto

BELOW Historic materials keep the past alive in this project. Reclaimed fir flooring, and adze-hewn log beams applied in a herringbone motif contribute to the authenticity at Sawtooth Mountain Ranch and are signatures of the architect and builder.
© Mark Darley/Esto

OPPOSITE TOP The unpretentious kitchen is a great place to rustle up a gourmet meal. There are no lavish gestures here just uncomplicated, clean spaces and as Tillotson-Miller states "We don't perform a lot of tricks—the trick is restraint." The kitchen cabinetry is from aged boards taken from the owner's farm in Georgia. They have been heavily waxed to bring out the rich amber tones.
© Mark Darley/Esto

OPPOSITE BOTTOM-LEFT The wall in this unique powder room at Sawtooth Ranch is made of corrugated steel roofing material that has been rusted, flattened, and sealed. A cauldron from the owners' farm in Georgia has been newly employed as a sink.
© Mark Darley/Esto

OPPOSITE BOTTOM-RIGHT The architect uses many outdoor rooms to create extra living rooms and transitional spaces. In all directions they take advantage of climates, light, and views, fully engaging the landscape. Colorful toboggans are unexpected as wall décor on this porch.
© Mark Darley/Esto

HOMAGE TO THE GREAT CAMP
ONTARIO, CANADA

ARCHITECT: **TIM BULLOCK** BUILDER: **BULLOCK LOG HOMES** INTERIOR DESIGN: **GREG PINCH**

The client was a fifth generation "cottager" seeking a departure from that style of home in the "lakes region" of Ontario, Canada. He looked to the nearby Adirondack Mountains for inspiration. The era of Great Camps from 1865 through the 1920s produced a broad offering of the finest rustic buildings in North America. This family envisioned a log cottage that would hark back to that time, and in the design and execution they strived to achieve a period feel in sensory details. They have succeeded, creating a warm lakefront retreat that shows a reverence for tradition.

Bullock Log Homes is one of the finest log and timber frame companies in North America. They are recognized for their fine execution of heavy timber roof systems and their use of indigenous northern white and red pine as the preferred building species. Located in Ontario, Canada, they were the builder of choice for this family on Redstone Lake. Nawakwa (In the Woods), as it is named, is built of round logs 12" to 18" in diameter in keeping with the scale of the topography. The logs are chinked, an unusual feature for this area. The contours of the structure are more Adirondack than lakes region, as witnessed in the wraparound porches, hipped roofs, round logs dressed in dark chocolate, and absence of a basement. All of the materials used were native: red and white pine logs, and granite. Antique hemlock floors were reclaimed, milled, and shellacked. Hand-forged nails and antique hardware were used wherever possible and added a layer of history to the new home.

In rustic design there is a direct correlation between the darkness of a color scheme and the degree of age achieved. At Nawakwa the rich chocolate brown logs mitigate any issue with the need for newer furnishings and modern conveniences.

OPPOSITE Hipped roofs, wraparound porches, and herringbone gable ends transport us to a different era and place—the Adirondacks circa 1920.
Photograph by stacey brandford photography

LEFT In an effort to conceal a large flat-screen television, the owner devised a touch pad system where the television pops up from a hidden door in the floor. The speakers are cleverly camouflaged by iron venting grates in the floor. All the electronics are completely invisible when not in use, to maintain the integrity of the period setting.
Photograph by stacey brandford photography

ABOVE The interior finish was completed by a "fanatic" who hand rubbed twelve coats of stain and wax, burnishing the logs to a warm and aged patina.

Photograph by stacey brandford photography

OPPOSITE A theatrical kitchen befitting a 1920s Craftsman home. It is difficult to impart a sense of age or rusticity to a kitchen; it needs to be practical and wipeable, so surfaces tend to be polished for that reason. Here, they have been successful in conveying both a rustic and period feel while maintaining utility. Quarter-sawn mission oak cabinets capped by soapstone counters are a suitably vintage combination for this home. To further instill the spirit of the 1920s a new stove was retrofitted with old parts to give the appearance of an antique.

Wiring a log home is labor intensive and awkward, it was a trick to imbed the halogen spotlights into the logs to create a little magic in this room. The wiring needed to be woven through an upper course of logs to be hidden from sight below.
Photograph by stacey brandford photography

RIGHT The wraparound porches are a tribute to the great camps of the Adirondacks, here outfitted with the owner's collection of Old Hickory furniture and a colorful canoe employed as wall décor. Deep overhangs keep the snow and rain away from the foundation and will increase the longevity of the cottage.
Photograph by stacey brandford photography

ABOVE This homey cottage bedroom represents the rustic ideal in sleeping quarters. The hickory bed, birch bark nightstand, Hudson Bay blankets, and fish mounts are set against a background of multi-hued stone.
Photograph by stacey brandford photography

A PORTFOLIO OF RUSTIC HOMES

ARTISANS ABODES

Creative people tend to feather their nests with things that will feed their spirit—their livelihood and inventiveness depends on it. The rustic homes in this section offer a peek into the personal spaces of a handful of artists and designers who have chosen rustic as a way of life.

The house is much larger than it appears from the entry. It is three stories tall and sits high on a slope thick with oak trees and rhododendron. The lower levels drop off of the back and cascade down the ridge. Skinned birch columns are a witty take on antebellum architecture. The rustic planters have been filled with wild growth gathered from the yard and gardens creating an untamed fall arrangement.

SOUTHERN COMFORT
NORTH CAROLINA

ARCHITECT: JACK DAVIS ARCHITECT
BUILDER: ASHE CONSTRUCTION, INC., KEITH ASHE
INTERIOR DESIGN: DOTTY TRAVIS

Dotty Travis, the founder and owner of Travis and Co., a purveyor of home furnishings, is a steel magnolia, the epitome of humor and grace. This design maven from Macon, Georgia, began collecting French antiques in 1969 and parlayed her interest into a business that showcases her many talents. The Travises built a mountain home in Highlands, North Carolina, to escape two demons: the summer heat of Atlanta and a hectic city life. Her son-in-law Jack Davis designed the provocative retreat, situated on a steep wooded ridge. It was executed by a builder that Travis says "is more than a builder, he is a mountain man with beautiful taste," a high compliment from this design doyenne. It is an entirely clever home expressed in perfect proportions. The 4000-square-foot structure is deceiving in size; it appears to be a simple box— in reality it is a jewel box. The house is a study in the economy of space; not an inch is wasted on hallways or connectors that consume coveted square footage. The 10-foot ceilings help with proportions and add volume to the rooms.

Travis wanted the home to resemble a primitive schoolhouse. A 19th-century front door, discovered in France, is the driving force behind the house design—a Southern mountain home with primitive French elements and rustic overtures. But it comes across as a purebred; Travis' flawless and unselfconscious taste is the overriding impression left. This is a woman who could gild a twig and apply it as molding to a barn board mirror to great effect. The couple bought an old cabbage barn and used every bit of it in this home. They instructed the builder to make two piles of boards, a reusable structural pile and an arts and crafts pile. The structural pile was used for items like cabinets and shutters while smaller remnants were relegated to mirror frames and the like.

Floors throughout the home are a mix of woods from old French railroad cars. Travis chose to have plaster over lath walls, an authentic but laborious process not often used today. It took newly trained plaster workers days to perfect the color and texture to the designer's satisfaction. Quirky but well-thought-out moldings seduce the eye. The ceiling in the great room features square timbers set in a course with a larger half-round log run perpendicular to it—a highly effective rustic touch. She designed an amusing chair rail that at first glance appears to be conventional but on closer inspection had been painted ochre with an applied peeled twig accent. Each room is a braiding of French antiques, mountain rustic, and American folk eclectic punctuated by a gypsy color palette that is underlined by Travis' liberal use of reds and ochres.

ABOVE This kitchen is perhaps one of the most charming rooms in the entire South. The floor is reclaimed 18th century terra-cotta tile from France, the island is a French shopkeeper's case and it is skirted in a patchwork created from different color-ways of the same fabric. The focal point of the room is a primitive fish painting by Atlanta artist Mary Klein. Shutters were assembled from wood salvaged from the cabbage barn. Together these elements form a naïve still life that is part southern rustic with a measure of country French.

ABOVE A folk art fireplace surround from Virginia allows for extended seasonal use on this porch dressed in autumnal colors. Chairs inscribed with mountain proverbs were plucked from a garage sale.

LEFT Mountain eclectic as illustrated in the master bath, an unlikely combination of taxidermy, stitchery, and toiletries.

OPPOSITE Bold, traditional, cabin colors—black and red—provide high contrast to the white walls in this stunning room that is used by Travis' grandchildren.

LEFT Travis sought drama in the powder room. The whimsical tableaux of the faux-painted countertop, half log bullnose, 18th-century Italian hand sconces, and a rough board mirror frame with a gilded twig accent was just the thing to offset this unusual fabric from Bergamo featuring trompe l'oeil framed landscapes.

BELOW LEFT One of the many interesting and clever details in this home: fieldstone inlaid into plaster as window trim.

BELOW RIGHT The finer points in this house are delightful and unstudied. Upon examination this porch rail detail is a disc cut from a branch with twig spoke-work to support the porch railings.

PORTRAIT OF AN ARTIST
NEW YORK

RENOVATION AND FURNITURE: BARNEY BELLINGER, SAMPSON BOG STUDIO

Barney Bellinger is arguably the preeminent and most sought after furniture builder and artist in the rustic world. His case goods incorporate all the woods have to offer; his showstopping twig mosaic and burl pieces are sure to be future classics. He and his family live on the fringe of the Adirondack Park in a series of buildings, the heart of which is his home, a cottage built in the 1930s and renovated by Bellinger over the last fifteen years. His business, Sampson Bog Studio, is located on the property in a series of charming workshops, one to warehouse the tools of his trade (roots, burls, twigs), one for mosaic twig work, and one for the painted finishes and glasswork that embellish his pieces. An additional hideaway cabin is tucked behind the studio. It is for Bellinger's daughter, Erin Estelle, who has started her own rustic picture frame business.

Bellinger is a man at peace in the wilderness, an avid fly fisherman who began his career as a sign painter. He is self-taught and has spent recent years using his painterly talent and passion for the outdoors to accentuate his furniture pieces. The Adirondack guide boat is an oft-repeated motif in his paintings. He is captivated by its fluid form, and has tacked countless images of this icon on the wall of his atelier.

OPPOSITE Bellinger at work in the twig cabin. The gable screen and railings have been woven out of burls and roots, a prologue to what lays inside.

ABOVE A room for reflection and inspiration, the artist's drawing room and office. It is a study in rustic mementos. The easel holds his most current work, an oil painting of an Adirondack guide boat.

RUSTIC REVISITED

RIGHT This angler's fishing cabinet is Bellinger's opus. The intricate display case took 18 months to build and is assembled in six articulated pieces. In a desire to broaden his repertoire this cabinet was made from both eastern and western materials. It is a textural piece encrusted in lodgepole pine burl, alder, leaded glass, antique bamboo fly rods, and antique German glass. The artist's nephew, Charley Brown, helped create this piece and has been an apprentice to Bellinger since he was twelve years old.

OPPOSITE TOP Sampson Bog Studios storage area for wood, twig, and burl, a warehouse for the best that nature has to offer.

OPPOSITE BOTTOM Bellinger fitting antique fly rods onto a mirror.

OPPOSITE RIGHT At every turn is a still life. Here a hallway displays a pleasing composition of fly-fishing paraphernalia.

A JEWEL IN THE WOODS

NORTH CAROLINA

INTERIOR DESIGN: LYNWOOD HALL

The name of the camp is Kituhwa, which is Cherokee for Gathering Place. The house sits on the original post-WW II settlement in the Blue Ridge Mountain town of Cashiers, North Carolina, on what once was Cherokee land. Lynwood Hall, the owner of this enchanting cottage, is a painter with a sensitivity to nature. He has retained a southern primitive aesthetic, carried with him from his Moultrie, Georgia, home. Hall's landscapes tell the story of the Carolina Mountains, as well as his passion for Provence, and his home has become the canvas for his inspiration. He has taken a hands-on approach to this cottage, which was built in the late 1950s as a simple saltbox and has been thoughtfully and painstakingly renovated over time. As in any long-term renovation this has been a game of addition and subtraction. Rooms have been added, walls moved, orange shag carpeting jettisoned and replaced by fine oriental rugs. The pine walls and ceiling beams are original to the house. The flooring is a combination of new and old heart pine plank. A détente has been reached between the desire to update outmoded architecture and the inclination to honor the past.

Hall's rendition of Southern rustic is highly personal. The home is a showcase for the artist's work, whether it is the pointillist mural in the dining room or the lamps made from various found vessels, they are exhibited with pride here. This Southern gentleman is a storyteller and a scavenger; there are few new things in this home, rather it is an accumulation of objects that have been resuscitated or reincarnated with new purpose. He has achieved a homey and primitive result.

OPPOSITE Lynwood Hall's well tended "garden" at Kituhwa, a jewel in the woods of Carolina. The basic cottage has been greatly enhanced by trellises and a veritable Eden of potted plants that intertwine with the architecture.

ABOVE AND RIGHT The comfortable great room at Kituhwa features a stacked Tennessee fieldstone fireplace that sits where a wall of glass sliders once were. The mason, Leland Hughey, was a third-generation stonemason who took his task to heart. Above the fireplace, a painting by Hall depicts a scene in Provence and coexists beautifully with other found objects, including the camel saddle that doubles as a footstool. Hall's grandmother made the quilt that hangs over the hickory stair rail. A neutral palette is effective and allows the exceptional rugs and artwork to play leading roles.

LEFT A wall collage above the bar showcases an assemblage of Hall's treasures and is a wonderful example of how to display one's collections. This is where the old camp kitchen stood.

OPPOSITE BOTTOM LEFT A naïve landscape abuts a primitive stone shower enclosure in this delightful bathroom. Note the chiseled wood plant stand emulates a tree trunk and serves as a lamp table.

LEFT Porches are a cultural icon in the South, an integral part of Southern life for over 200 years. The porch at Hall's feels like a tree house. Ceiling rafters became lattice work for the painted espalier. Repurposed prizes abound: elm red lacquered Chinese chairs, olive jars made into lamps, a cog from a wooden wheel as sculpture.

BELOW Heart pine paneling in the dining room was taken in its entirety from a home built in the 1880s at nearby Pinehurst, North Carolina. The mural was painted in the impressionist manner by Hall and depicts Big Sheepcliff Mountain, which hovers behind his home. A work table from a frame shop has found new life as Hall's dining table.

91

ASIAN FUSION IN THE ADIRONDACKS
NEW YORK

INTERIOR DESIGN: GRETCHEN BELLINGER

Textile designer Gretchen Bellinger is the lady of this dramatic house. She is known for the refined application of natural fibers featured in her sophisticated line of home-furnishing fabrics. This delightful cottage on Long Lake in the Adirondacks was acquired in 1988, and Bellinger has burnished it into a showplace that doesn't appear to have been renovated as much as polished. The concise structure is well balanced, a screened-in porch runs the full length of the house and anchors the twin dormers and gable that project from the steep roof. Inside, the cottage has a skeletal rib work of open studs that frame her many collections. Consequently it is not insulated and can be used only in the summer months.

There is a pleasing symmetry to this home, which, coupled with her finely edited furniture arrangements, is simply stunning. Bellinger was profoundly influenced by a semester in Japan as a young student and it has manifested itself throughout the house. The Asian overtones are an unusual juxtaposition to the campy stage set. She began the sprucing-up process sixteen years ago by scrubbing the endless planes of Douglas fir board-and-bead woodwork—it had never been shellacked and when it cleaned up to a beautiful warm gold tone, she was inspired to press on. In the business of interior design, a home is never really finished, improvements continue in a series of ongoing projects and upgrades. Such is the case in Long Lake as this "woman of the cloth" is constantly reinventing her retreat. More recent efforts reflect her newest collection of Asian-inspired fabrics.

OPPOSITE The quiet presence of this cottage reveals nothing of the theatre that is carried on inside.

LEFT Symmetry at its finest in Bellinger's great room. The original fireplace is framed by two Isamu Noguchi paper shade floor lamps. The lady of the house has a well-stamped passport; the coffee table was a doctor's examining table brought back from Japan. The heavily grained oak round game table is an antique Mission piece from the Limbert Company and provides an informal alternative to the dining room.

LEFT The folly of an important Empire chest flanked by elaborate handblown Murano glass sconces and crowned with a deer head, all set on open studs make an absurd yet highly effective vignette.

OPPOSITE TOP Taxidermy never looked so good. Much of it was bequeathed to the present owner from the previous one. The Japanese silk cocoon baskets complete the composition and become artwork when placed in tandem with deer mounts.

OPPOSITE BOTTOM Pared down décor, strategically placed Chinese pieces, and quiet color give the Asian bedroom a Zen-like aura. It's an unlikely pairing of Chinoiserie and camp. The print over the bed was made for Gretchen by artist Robert Natkin. All of the fabrics used in this home are from the Bellinger Collection and have exotic labels like *Golden Apples*, *Gibraltar*, and *Pasha*.

ABOVE Taupe is Bellinger's color of choice. She has been generous in its application in all intensities both outside and in. The schoolhouse chairs on pegs are a humorous wink at the Shakers and provide extra seating for the porch.

OPPOSITE The artist has used taxidermy as a bridge from clean country cottage to rustic as is evident in the master bath at this camp.

HIGH COUNTRY RUSTIC

NORTH CAROLINA

ARCHITECT: Shamburger Design Studio, Wayland Shamburger, AIA
BUILDER: Trillium Construction INTERIOR DESIGN: Ginny Stine Interiors, Ginny Stine Romano, ASID

High on a plateau in the Smoky Mountains of North Carolina, Florida interior and fabric designer Ginny Stine and her husband Richard Romano found relief from the sweltering summer heat. At and altitude of 4,000 feet in a forest dense with locust, old-growth oak, and massive rhododendron, the Stine Romanos built a sophisticated retreat they call The Twigs. At first glance it appears to be a simple one-story multi-gabled home, but the slope at the back of the house drops off precipitously and the house becomes a more compelling three-story lodge with stacked porches, annexed forms, and multiple rooflines. Subtle but powerful decorative details distinguish The Twigs from other rustic homes in the area.

This home is what I would call High Country Rustic, a southern, ultra-refined version of its more musty and rough cousin Adirondack style. Stine's husband was raised in the mountains of Europe and the mandate was to convey a gutsy rusticity associated with Bavarian hunting lodges without the darkness traditionally associated with this genre. They wanted the interior to have the openness of a barn, which led them to post and beam construction. Additionally, the spaces needed to leave latitude for playing with the furniture and the decorative arrangements for which Ginny is known.

The strongly defined interiors are a study in placement. Whether it is a collection of early-19th-century pinecone prints or the careful arrangement of a Russian bronze desk set, nothing has been left to chance. The backdrop for these vignettes is v-groove pine board washed in a buttercream stain that segues to natural and heavily marked wood boards.

OPPOSITE The exterior of The Twigs is sheathed in a pleasing combination of "feather board" (aka brainstorm) and board and batten. A craftsman detail, the quill batten, has been added for interest. Stacked Tennessee fieldstone is wrapped around the home and is used for the fireplaces. The consummate designer, Stine gathered blue spruce needles and had the paint store computer match the stain used on the exterior. Gable screens and posts are locust trees, and the rail work is easily identified as laurel because of its consistent diameter. Laurel is the Southern version of cedar. It can be woven in the same manner and lends itself to railings and furniture.

LEFT In the great room at The Twigs the dark tone of the furniture plays off of the knots in the pine boards. The floor and ceiling are the same value; the former is covered in a textured sisal which is a neutral setting for the tableaux. An inveterate shopper and collector, Ginny began her extensive collection of Black Forest carved pieces when she purchased a seven-piece antique parlor suite years ago. It is covered in a fabric with a pinecone motif designed by Stine. The Tapis Verdure is likely late-17th-century French.

LEFT Post and beam construction modifies the verticality of the space in the library and imparts the desired feel of a barn. Majestic bronze deer hold court in the monarch pose above the library, guarding Stine's extensive collection of blue-and-white 18th- and 19th-century Chinese export porcelain. The painting over the mantel is by Swedish impressionist Frans Eric Gard, the Indian bronze is a recast of a piece by Phinster Procter (the original took first place in Paris World's Fair in 1900).

OPPOSITE In the twin bedroom, 12" rough-hewn pine was put through a special process to achieve a timeworn look. First it was stained dark brown, then painted in butter cream, lightly sanded, and coated in clear varnish. The painted metal beds are antiques from a Russian dacha circa the 1750s. Cornices have been cleverly fashioned from old crazy quilts.

LEFT A dramatic billiard table is the centerpiece for the Tartan Room. The Brunswick table is painted in faux twig and mountain scenes with antler button rivets applied for dimension. This is an outside-in room. Stine selected exterior finishes like the locust log posts and porch lights to achieve the look. The rug design was a collaboration between Stine and manufacturer Lacey Champion. A hired man's bed with tartan-covered mattress doubles as a place for the peanut gallery behind the game table.

LEFT Even the powder room sports an engaging collection, in this case tramp art frames and Transferware china. The 19th-century American dressing table has been converted into a commode by drilling a hole in an antique bowl and plumbing it.

BELOW Stine's master bath is a woodland glade compliments of Brunschwig and Fils leafy wallpaper, slate floor, butterfly granite, and custom black cabinetry that has an almost imperceptible undercoat of green.

OPPOSITE A serene porch with a series of hickory rockers framed by a rail of locust posts and laurel balustrade is the embodiment of Southern rustic.

Photograph by Roger Wade © 2001/Ginny Stine Interiors, Mill Creek Post & Beam

LOG LIVING

"Log cabins are the quintessential American building type. They have transcended mere nostalgia to become icons of our national past. Given the depth of our affection for them, it's hardly surprising that Americans are still building them." says Richard Moe, the president of the National Trust for Historic Preservation. What began as unassuming shelter has grown to multi-story lodges. The log home these days can take the shape of a 400-square-foot guest cabin or a 10,000-square-foot ski house.

The following homes represent a cross section of North American log dwellings—from cabin to lodge. Throughout this book there are a number of other log homes that have been categorized under a different heading. They all bear attention for their unique adaptation of trees.

Ingredients for the quintessential Western rustic great room: lofty ceiling, lodgepole pine log work, tobacco-stained, rough-sawn pine flooring, local river rock fireplace, and the requisite taxidermy. The owner is of mid-European descent, and brought in many antique pieces lending this room a decidedly Alpine flavor.

A LOG CABIN TRANSFORMED
COLORADO

ARCHITECT: VAG, INC. ARCHITECTS AND PLANNERS
BUILDER: BECK BUILDING COMPANY INTERIOR DESIGN: WESTERN TRADITIONS, VICKI WARD

In the 1980s an original, unassuming cabin was built on a mountainside in Colorado as a simple gray log structure with small windows. Two decades and a load of inspiration later a handsome retreat emerged. The new owner hoped to reinforce the regional flavor and chose to renovate by continuing in the log vernacular. The exterior of the house was reconfigured, the facade favorably altered by a new entrance, multiple rooflines, dormers, and larger windows. The builder faced a tremendous challenge in tying the new logs in to existing log work—coursing had to be matched, rooflines fitted, and new electrical wiring routed through the cabin walls. The interior was gutted, rooms were added, fireplaces changed, and ceiling heights maneuvered. The net result is a charming home in a resort community.

Transitions in ceiling heights and materials define the spaces of this house. The two great rooms with soaring ceilings are linked by the original kitchen, which remained approximately 8' high. A stone entry floor segues easily into a distressed wood floor to delineate the formal great room. By varying floor materials throughout the house, individual living areas are acknowledged. The décor is ski-house eclectic, but punctuated with the bright color and energetic pattern of painted Bavarian antiques against the strong linear effect created by the log chinking.

An ordinary log cabin was reconfigured and transformed into a winner. The roof was vastly altered by the addition of a new great room, dormer windows, and copper shingles. A talented team of architect and builder made these modifications seamless, successfully matching size, course, and color to the logs of the original structure. The stonework is a rounded and smooth river rock, indigenous but not often seen.

A vaulted ceiling mirroring the proportion of the great room demarcates an annex addition beyond the kitchen that links these two spaces. A change in flooring from rough-sawn pine to white oak supports the transition. The red cabinets are a holdover from the original house and are painted, patinated, and twigged in the rustic folk manner. A substantial and generously scarred mesquite dining table has served past and present incarnations of the house.

ABOVE LEFT It was necessary to rebuild the stairway using full-scribe log stringers and treads to accommodate a carpet runner. The intricate railing is a cast bronze bullwhip with branch balusters created in sections by Peter Fillerup. The pieces were shipped from Utah, assembled on site, then merged with log newel posts and stringers.

ABOVE RIGHT A beguiling cast bronze branch treatment for the front door was created by Peter Fillerup of Wild West Designs.

LEFT Custom hand-painted beds rendered in a leaping stag theme grace the guest room. Transitions were important in this house, they have successfully segued from log to plaster and back again throughout the interior.

NORTHWOODS LODGE
WISCONSIN

BUILDER: **TED MOODY**   INTERIOR DESIGN: **NORTHPOINT LODGE COLLECTION**

Near the Chequamegon National Forest of Wisconsin sits placid Spider Lake. It is located near a town called Hayward, which existed primarily for the lumbermen who forested the land in the 1920s. With the help of Hank Smith, a Native American, Ted Moody built this lodge in 1923 for city friends and paying guests to come visit and fish. After a number of incarnations it was reopened as a B & B in 1990. In 2000 new owners Jim Kerkow and Craig Mason stepped up to the plate and have applied their charming brand of rustic to the grand lodge, making it an inviting, adventurous, and romantic retreat for Northwoods travelers. The inn's motto "Here There Is No Time" says it all.

OPPOSITE The lodge was built of native logs in the manner of the Adirondack Great Camps. The dark log interior remains as it was in the '20s, but has been beautifully restored, as have many of the antiques and accents. Jim and Craig have filled the lodge with a kitschy combination of vintage accessories and some serious artwork—all ingredients for an alluring rustic experience.

Photograph by maxhaynes.com

ABOVE At Spider Lake Lodge the proprietors have created a potpourri of memorabilia, new acquisitions, and delicious finds blended with significant antiques. The waxed dark wood logs set horizontally break into a herringbone pattern and promote an atmosphere of old camp.

Photograph by maxhaynes.com

ABOVE A more colorful or comfortable porch could not be found. Cushions dressed in vintage blankets sit on a 1920s gothic rattan settee. The seating is kept in good company by painted folk pieces and campy details.

Photograph by maxhaynes.com

OPPOSITE TOP The owners have licensed a collection of home furnishings under the name *The Northpoint Lodge Collection*, which offers the best of what's available in rustic décor. Each piece has been selected to convey the comfort and serenity of the lodge and lake setting.

The fireplace is original to the building and is of local river rock identifiable by its pleasing rounded face.

Photograph by maxhaynes.com

RIGHT Spider Lake is renowned for its superb muskie fishing. Here a sizable trophy of the species completes a rustic vignette.

Photograph by maxhaynes.com

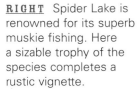

ABOVE Birkenbeiner, one of the guest rooms at the lodge, is the embodiment of Northwoods décor. A folky bedstead and a bold black and red scheme are enveloped by knotty pine wall and ceiling planks—a rustic failsafe for any region.

Photograph by maxhaynes.com

OPPOSITE BOTTOM
Old water skis find a
new use as a chair
back—an amusing take
on the classic Adirondack
throne of summer.

Photograph by maxhaynes.com

ABOVE Bear's Den has
been decked out as a log
cabin with all of the
appropriate fittings: bear
skin, Hudson Bay point
blankets, and vivid color.

Photograph by maxhaynes.com

OPPOSITE This cabin was given new life by the artful use of large overhangs, exposed timber, and rusticated stonework. It achieved a greater presence by the addition of a splayed entry stair and the figured log corner posts, creating a curvilinear impression. The cascading stair spreads the visual load of the building to the ground.

Photograph by Jared Hoke

ABOVE The piano room and living area is a clean, uncomplicated space ideal for practice or performance for this musical family. "Even contemporary things look old in this context," Hillbrand observes. The exposed bark-on rafters and trusses that frame the room are part of the original structure.

Photograph by Nick Gorski/NKG Studios

SETTLER'S CABIN REDUX

MINNESOTA

ARCHITECT: **SALA ARCHITECTS, INC., KATHERINE HILLBRAND, AIA, CID**
BUILDER/RENOVATION: **NICK HEINEN CONSTRUCTION AND JOHN NIEMANN**

This unpretentious home perches on a wooded bluff overlooking the St. Croix River in Minnesota. This area outside of St. Paul is one of America's protected Wild and Scenic Waterways. The original cabin was constructed in 1913, using round logs with the bark on and oakham chinking, a style commonly used by Swedish settlers. The original one-room log cabin was annexed and appended over the years but remained dysfunctional for the needs of the current owners. The architects were called in to vastly increase the space by adding bedrooms, bathrooms, a larger kitchen, and a second entry.

The design team was sensitive to the historic character of the building; they were challenged to maintain the low profile and original street facade but to double the living space. Architect Katherine Hillbrand specializes in handcrafted timber buildings, and here she found the opportunity for expansion underground by excavating below the existing structure and extending only one portion of the cabin while maintaining the same roof pitch. They were able to carve out three bedrooms and two baths where a partial basement had been.

Best use was made of the existing stone foundation, which was supplemented with stonework in native limestone. Large overhangs, masonry, and exposed timbers rejuvenate the rustic legacy of the original cabin. Despite its recent transformation, the building has retained its humble charm and remains a much recognized and beloved landmark in this quaint town.

On the interior, to bring this cabin up to snuff, the contractor refinished existing floors and used recycled Douglas fir to marry new with old. That spirit was retained in the furnishing of the cabin. Deep roof overhangs and a densely wooded site dictated that the interior palette be light. This set off the antiques the family placed throughout the house, adding a dose of history to this clever cabin.

ABOVE The bedroom wall was part of the original basement foundation, and the room was previously accessed by a trap door. The limestone makes an interesting backdrop for the bed, and an arched doorway to the bathroom lends a sense of grotto to this subterranean space.

Photograph by Nick Gorski/NKG Studios

OPPOSITE TOP Kitchen cabinetry was built from old cherry wood and topped with black slate counters, a fitting choice for a period kitchen. Small low windows above the counter might look like an error but are strategically placed to look down the embankment for a glorious river view.

Photograph by Chris Koch

OPPOSITE BOTTOM A reading nook was created from the original exterior log wall of the cabin. A window previously occupied the space where the bookshelf was built.

Photograph by Katherine Hillbrand

ROCKY MOUNTAIN SKI HOUSE
COLORADO

DESIGN: **TAB ASSOCIATES, TAB BONIDY** CONTRACTOR: **RESORT CONCEPTS** INTERIORS: **BY OWNER**

When building on the side of a mountain you either build up or down. In this case the site, in the tony resort of Bachelor Gulch in the Rocky Mountains, was a ski-in/ski-out home on a steep upward slope. To avoid hiking up a full flight of stairs to arrive at the main living space the foundation was broken up into many terraced spaces. This mountainside home is about scale—the relationship of mountains to logs to people. It walks the line of overstepping proportions but is successful in its relevance to all three. There was concern that the log framework, supplied by Bitterroot Log Homes from Montana, would overwhelm the space. The Douglas fir trusses were artfully executed in a scissor formation with a king post to avoid eclipsing the mountain and sky views. It took seven flatbed trucks of exterior logs to get the job done.

The owner wanted a true great room and was granted his wish—the room encompasses a sizeable kitchen, a breakfast bar area, a proper dining room, and an expansive seating area.

OPPOSITE This stone and log home is a commanding presence on the slope of a ski resort. The steeply gabled roofs of the garage, entry, and main body of the house create the impression of individual lodges, and are anchored by a tapered stone foundation.

LEFT The massive front door made from mesquite is in keeping with the Bunyanesque scale of this log home. It measures 9' high by 8' wide.

LEFT The clients wanted a great room with lodge proportions while maintaining a warm and comfortable home that wouldn't diminish the human experience. The monochromatic color scheme draws the eye to the textural features of the room, including a hickory accent table, fancy feather shades, taxidermy and animal-skin rugs, and an impressive antler chandelier. The massive fireplace is comprised of 65,000 pounds of Colorado Moss Rock.

OPPOSITE TOP Some of the most expensive square footage in the country is in this area and homeowners here are compelled to use every bit of it for living space. There is no basement in this home—this room was designated as the bunkhouse for the grandchildren. When talking vacation house, the more heads in the beds, the better.

OPPOSITE BOTTOM The inventive powder room features walls and a vanity that have been sheathed in the bark rind (reverse side) of a white birch tree. Twig was applied without restraint to the mirror frame. The interior walls of the log home have been troweled with plaster followed by a second coat that was applied with recycled carpet squares.

The five onion domes for the Russian House at Topridge were constructed in Connecticut by Luckey and Company and trucked up to the Adirondacks. They could not be brought in by road but had to be ferried across the lake on a barge and hoisted up the ridge by a crane. The spectacle was met with applause. A special furnace was built to steam the shingles so they would conform to the dome's contours.

Five hundred pieces of mahogany were required to create the substantial front door that was designed by the architect. The relief design depicts the interlocking forms that were the floor plan for this building. Filigree trim for the windows was sketched in elaborate shapes strung together then scanned, computerized, and cut with a laser.

FANTASY RUSTIC

I magination unbridled, whimsy run rampant, these homes are originals. They are visionary, thought provoking, and in some cases cerebral—all are experiential. They have taken rustic to the brink of reality by reinventing it. For their owners these dream homes are a source of joy, amusement, and great pride.

WILDERNESS WONDERLAND

NEW YORK

DESIGN: ARCHITECT OF FEATURED BUILDINGS: RICHARD GIEGENGACK
BUILDER: TISSOT CONSTRUCTION CO.: CHRIS TISSOT, JIM BRUSH, TOM LAMB, TOM HUNT
INTERIOR DESIGN: ROGERS-FORD L.C. ARCHITECTURE-DESIGN

Camp Topridge is held in high esteem in the company of the Great Camps of the Adirondacks. This grande dame of compounds was built in 1897 and purchased in 1920 by the cereal heiress Marjorie Merriweather Post to be used as a summer retreat. After many years of derelict ownership the compound was salvaged by its current owner, who has restored it beyond its former glory. The camp is a veritable playground, and the joy the owner has taken in creating such a fantastic scenario is evident at every turn. Topridge sits high on a hogback ridge, overlooking a quiet lake on one side and twin ponds on the other. It was an irksome piece of land to build on, requiring a great amount of fortitude and luck to pull it off. There are forty structures on the property, eleven of them are sleeping cabins. The guests are encouraged to gather for meals in the main lodge, thus the cabins are not outfitted with dining facilities.

There was no true master plan for the property but rather a metamorphosis took place. Buildings were renovated one at a time. The impetus for the compound was a painting depicting a Russian "Village of Spires" and in a vague way, this drove the selection of style for each building. One building was modeled after the Norwegian stave church; another was Alpine in inspiration, and another clearly Russian. The property is unified by repeated references to these northern European habitats and by the choice of log and stone as the primary building materials, maintaining the Adirondack spirit. What was asked of the craftspeople on this project was a lot, what they delivered was more. There was a mutual respect for talent and nature, and the outcome is nothing less than spectacular. This team was well versed in rustic architecture (they are among the finest in the country) and with Topridge the bar has been raised for others to explore the outer limits of this genre. Here we show some of the newer major buildings on the compound.

Marjorie Merriweather Post had erected a dacha as a tribute to her third husband, Joseph E. Davies, who was ambassador to Russia in the 1930s, so the new Russian building completed seven decades later is the logical progeny. Maple Island Log Homes fabricated the log shells. The complete log structures were built in Michigan, numbered log by log, then shipped to Topridge and reassembled. The Russian building was a feat of engineering; its plan derived from nine nested octagons requiring forty intersections where a wall plane would change. This geometry presented many more complex log joints than most log structures and the skill of Maple Island's craftsmen (carving all the joints with hand-held chain saws) produced an extraordinary result.

The new boathouse was conceived to take the place of a timeworn one. It is a formidable presence on this lake and a reminder of the power of nature to inspire man. Its height is based on clearance for the boats housed here and the need for guest rooms above. The lakes of the Adirondack Park are ideal for boating; navigating the waterways is a large part of summer recreation here.

There are many other new or improved buildings on the compound (a stone church and vintage soda fountain among them). Though each has a distinct personality, there is a cohesiveness to Topridge. The buildings are linked not only by footpaths but also by a common appreciation of the history of this property as the wonderland of the Adirondack Park.

OPPOSITE AND ABOVE
The volume and sense of space in the buildings at Topridge is noteworthy. In the new buildings the ceilings are high and the main rooms large; this great room in the Russian House illustrates the point. It is also a masterpiece of fine woodworking.

The intricate railings and log-end details have been hand carved and the log siding has all been hand finished. This room glows. The furnishings are well chosen but are subordinate to the structural elements.

RIGHT The domes were uniquely, specifically engineered and built for this building with the intent that the inner cavity would be decorative and exposed to view from within. It is a compelling focal point in the room; a kaleidoscopic image is created by the polygonal symmetry.

ABOVE The current dining room was once an outside porch, now converted to this captivating dining room at the main lodge. Ms. Post amassed a vast collection of Native American artifacts; these baskets with decorated rawhide collars were transformed into pendant lights. The outside/in brainstorm siding has been painted dark green and is a rich backdrop to the rustic appointments.

OPPOSITE The very Scandinavian master suite in the building known as Lothrop is based on the architecture of Norwegian stave churches. The cabinet that divides the seating area from the sleeping level has been embellished with a scene of the lake this camp sits on.

RUSTIC REVISITED

RIGHT A holdover from the Post era, this remarkable stairway has been painted in vivid hieroglyphics and is flanked by totem poles from Ms. Post's collection. An inverted woven basket of Native American attribution has been repurposed as the ceiling fixture.

BELOW The spectacular new boathouse at Topridge could fall into the category of Baroque rustic. Great attention was given to the size of the stones; these granite behemoths from a local quarry were used for the cut stone skirting foundation. Giegengack designed the round stone portals as a nautical, yet rustic touch. Much of the elaborate stonework at Topridge was done by Lamphere Contracting.

Shadows cast from the log and twig work are a powerful element considered by the architect in the design process. The flared trunks and woven branches of cedar emulate the dramatic twig work on the older boathouse that remains on the property (see page 15).

ABOVE The ultra-rustic exterior of the boathouse (see page 128) acts as camouflage for the sleek interior. The designer's schematic for this inviting bedroom demanded a clean palette of black and white with few natural forms. The architect added rope insets into the window trim and a carved rope detail on the doors to enhance the nautical theme. A history buff and inveterate collector, the owner displays the clan tartans and travel trunks once owned by the Duke of Windsor.

BELOW This playful bathroom in the boathouse could be on a large luxury liner.

ADIRONDACK ECLECTIC
NEW YORK

ARCHITECTURAL AND INTERIOR DESIGN:
ELIZABETH STEWART DESIGN, LLC, ELIZABETH STEWART
ARCHITECT: REED A. MORRISON BUILDER: BAIRD EDMONDS BUILDER, INC.

History was checked at the door when this captivating camp was built—the order of the day was to design a playful and quirky mountain perch in the High Peaks region of the Adirondacks.

Although the schematic encompassed a compound of structures, Lean-To Camp was built in an unorthodox sequence. The owners lived in a lean-to that was original to the property while the garage and guest house (Annex) were built, then they moved into the Annex while the family quarters were completed. This project had a big agenda and it was crucial that any kinks be worked out before the "big performance" (aka the family quarters).

The location is Keene Valley, settled in the tucks and folds of the Adirondacks surrounded by mountains with names like Gothics, Haystack, and Cascade. Architectural and interior designer Elizabeth Stewart nestled the three buildings into a slope with lofty views of Wolf Jaws and its neighboring ridge. The structures were arranged with an Adirondack point of view. The buildings are private but accessible to each other via footpaths. They are visually unified by a shared aesthetic that acknowledges local rustic tradition in the form of a classic Keene Valley farmhouse.

The Annex posed a challenge; the owner wanted each guest suite to have a fireplace, sleeping porch, and bathroom—a tall order and a design conundrum. It was in books on American cottage and farmhouse architecture that Stewart found her solution: the cruciform. This early church "T" formation was the basic layout for the house form in America. She tucked the sleeping porches in the corners of the cross to accommodate all of the special requirements.

The family quarters are pure Keene Valley vernacular as seen in the scale, material specifications, and windows. Stewart chose to shake up the primitive form and proportion associated with the genre and give it a lean look to impress a vertical notion. This is an eccentric Gothic American farmhouse sporting a steep 12 on 12 pitch roof, where a cedar shake plane dives into galvanized steel. The roofs accentuate the pleasant line of the architecture and soften the impact of the buildings on the landscape. Stewart developed a color system for the house: she took bark to have it computer matched and has used up to twelve permutations of this grayish-green as a common refrain both inside and out. The lacquer red of the windows is an exclamation mark and is run like a thread through the interior of the home, becoming the warp for the remaining weft of color used.

The interiors are decidedly eclectic—historically a license taken with Adirondack camps. This fantastic melange highlights the client's love of Bavaria, Scotland, and the Adirondacks. Assertive colors were chosen to stand up to the strong landscape and bleak winter light. The scale of the house could absorb the use of these fanciful hues: red, ochre, purple, and green—saturated colors that are a departure for a camp, unexpected choices and combinations that are intended to inspire. The verticality of the rooms and color palette play with perception and consequently the interiors have a "through-the-looking-glass" quality to them.

Distinct geometric shapes form a medley of roofs on the main house. The broken pitch pays homage to the roofs of the Alpine lodge. The facades of Lean-To Camp are an excellent example of mixing rustic sidings—they have successfully incorporated board and batten, brainstorm, and slab siding.

RIGHT A soaring entry provides an enchanting welcoming point. The foyer's airy glass panels and pitched ceiling suggest a birdcage. The birch bark panels, feral twig chandelier, and filigree arches hint at the woodland setting. This precise tone of purple was required as relief from the wood floor and walls elsewhere in the camp and was a departure from red. Twig work throughout the house is by Gary Brewer. The table was commissioned by the owner from George Jaques, a Keene Valley legend and third-generation rustic furniture builder.

OPPOSITE TOP New rustic and high energy collide in this dazzling great room. A powerful red, black, and white color scheme prevails and is underscored by a massive entertainment center built on site and painted in the Bavarian folk manner. Wildlife in the form of zebra skins, taxidermy, and monkey lamps are bold punctuations and provide texture, pattern, and a rustic reference for this stylish diorama. The room's hyperbolic elevations created the need for a decorative detail to break up the verticals and humanize the scale. A twig gallery with large pinecone finials was applied for that purpose. The brilliant lacquer red coffered ceiling with herringbone plates and bark accents is a composition often repeated in Stewart's projects. Two enormous iron chandeliers provide both symmetry and scale for this room.

LEFT The Mad Hatter would have enjoyed tea in this dining room where raucous color mingles with magnified scale and a wild riff is taken on a Tudor period fireplace. Flared root pedestals support a table that has a birch bark and twig apron. Oval frames hold antique prints from the McKenney and Hall portrait gallery of Native Americans. At the turn of the last century a fascination with Native American culture was evident in the souvenirs shipped back to the camps of the Adirondacks; rugs, beaded garments, tribal artwork were all too uncivilized for a main residence but deemed interesting and colorful as ornaments in a vacation home.

ABOVE An unusual finish schedule dictated that the same wood be used on the floor and walls throughout the interiors. In the kitchen they have been treated with a forest green paint. This verdant floor, leafy green cabinets, and ochre upper wall mimic the landscape painting that hangs above the fireplace. The handy log bin below the hearth is a clever solution to the messy holders that occupy valuable space. A primitive chicken-rail twig plate rack encircles the room as a witty architectural comment. The chairs, with quatrefoil cutouts and woven rawhide seats, are from neighboring Quebec. Counters are made of a textured, fired granite.

OPPOSITE BOTTOM The mudroom at Lean-To Camp is impressive for its combination of style and utility. In a region that boasts three enjoyable seasons, two Winter Olympics, forty six peaks to climb, lakes, rivers, and streams to play in and countless other outdoor attractions it is imperative to keep a full complement of gear available. Hooks, nooks, and shelving allow for maximum storage and easy access for the call of the wild.

ABOVE An unconventional Russian blue was designated for this guest suite in the Annex. Beaverboard (aka Homeosote) walls, previously considered the humble relation of Sheetrock, have been elevated to higher status with the brilliant blue. Adirondack closets consisting of a curtain, pole, and shelf were devised out of need for storage as well as a nostalgic camp gesture. In the true rustic tradition, much of the furniture in the Annex was pulled from here and there and happily resuscitated.

INSPIRED BY NATURE

NEW YORK

ARCHITECT: **Shope Reno Wharton Associates** INTERIOR DESIGN: **Gomez Associates, Mariette Himes Gomez**
BUILDER: **SBE Builders, Stephen Epifano**

A path of cyclopean glacial stones lead to this extraordinary home in New York State. It sits on a rolling tract of land with a varied landscape of forests, hills, and meandering stone fences. The house teases with branches and glimpses of long views through porch railings, but does not show its hand immediately. This structure focuses on the potential in man's relationship to nature—our ability to appreciate and take inspiration from light, form, color, scale, and other visual riches that nature offers. The client would find moments in nature and request the architectural equivalent: in one instance he showed the architect a photograph of a pond with fall leaves and asked that he capture the essence of the light, color, and movement in a space within his home. This was translated into an upper hallway.

As architecture the house is both simple and complex; it is arguably the most avant-garde and intellectual expression of rustic in the country. As an example, at a glance the interior walls are made of long cherry boards harvested from the site. A more careful look reveals that the boards are carefully arranged by width and color, the widest darkest boards at the floor level. The boards diminish in width and color as they rise toward the ceiling, creating the illusion of the entasis of a Greek column. The floor plan accommodates the lifestyle of a modern family. Rooms are open to one another and to the outdoors, removing barriers between the house and nature. The experience of being in this house is visceral and all-encompassing; the house changes with the light from hour to hour.

A specialized work force was bought in for this job and encouraged to cull as much of the building materials as possible from the site. The craftsmen needed to subordinate their individuality and adopt a more holistic approach to problem solving—they all rose to the challenge and set their sights on the final solution. They chose to cooperate with nature rather than dominate it; natural elements suggested the design solutions and were held in reverence.

Furnishings are underplayed, taking a backseat to the architectural drama. A monochromatic, neutral color scheme headlined by fine antiques allows Mother Nature to take center stage.

Nature takes on a mystical air on this porch. The gnarled, aromatic cedar tree posts are set on stone blocks that are part of the granite ledge that lies underneath the mahogany deck.
Photograph courtesy Charles Lindsay and Shope, Reno, Wharton Associates

The oculus at the gable end of the house is masked in a maelstrom of branches—a remarkable gesture of rustic twiggery. Much of the wood used both inside and out was procured, cut, and milled on the property. Black walnut boards were scribed for a soft-edged sheathing. American white oak was employed for the vertical base paneling.

Photograph courtesy Charles Lindsay and Shope, Reno, Wharton Associates

OPPOSITE The horizontal rays of the sun penetrate into the core of the house though large oval windows framed in woven sticks at opposite ends of the house. The walls of the house act as a sundial. At sunrise on the winter solstice, the shadows are in perfect alignment with each other and the visual axis to the lake. Through these tandem oculi light fills the great room, filtering down through cedar branches to cast soft shadows across the space.
Photograph courtesy Charles Lindsay and Shope, Reno, Wharton Associates

ABOVE This house is a rustic tour de force. The children's wing is a study in texture; there is not a surface that does not engage the senses. The feel of the pillowed floorboards on the feet is luxurious.
Photograph courtesy Charles Lindsay and Shope, Reno, Wharton Associates

ABOVE An upper hallway gallery elucidates the experience of living inside a piece of fine art. The railing is woven from mountain laurel. The chandelier, created by Steve Joslyn, depicts the four seasons and provides light for the gallery.

Photograph courtesy Charles Lindsay and Shope, Reno, Wharton Associates

DETAIL AT LEFT The twisting shapes of the cherry trees on the property create a rhythm when seen collectively. It is a condition unique to this species and would have been lost on milled boards. The architects wanted to feature this pattern in the house. The 40-foot trees were cut into long boards with the edges left natural. Each plank was used in full length and width and scribed one to the next, leaving the shape of the tree fully expressed in the floor. A tactile quality was added by hand-scraping each board, leaving a crown.

Photograph courtesy Charles Lindsay and Shope, Reno, Wharton Associates

ABOVE A large thicket of dead mountain laurel stood on the property. The growth had been killed by a drought. These magnificent trees became the railings for the house. These skeletons take on a sculptural quality, which is magnified when light cascades through the gnarled branches. Each root burl precisely fit the treads and serendipity provided exactly the right number to complete the job.
Photograph courtesy Charles Lindsay and Shope, Reno, Wharton Associates

LEFT Enormous cedars had grown around generations of barbed wire. The design team found locations for these special pieces of wood to allow their stories to be told over and over. Here the trees are woven together in an arbor that forms the porch columns.
Photograph courtesy Charles Lindsay and Shope, Reno, Wharton Associates

LITTLE JEWELS

Good design doesn't need to be fancy or oversized. These little retreats offer just the right amount of panache and soulfulness to make them profoundly appealing refuges. Often they are part of a grander scheme, the preferred nesting spot on a larger compound. Other times they are lone rangers, their own destination of choice. Because of their size, these little jewels are easily managed, a priceless commodity for hectic lives.

The concise guest cabin has two bedrooms, living and kitchen area, and a bathroom. The earthy tones of the antiqued logs and rusted Cor-ten roof lend authenticity and help it blend into the landscape.

A RIVER RUNS THROUGH IT
COLORADO

ARCHITECT: **DUANE PIPER** BUILDER: **BECK BUILDING COMPANY** INTERIOR DESIGN: **SLIFER DESIGNS, ANDREA GEORGOPOLIS**

The romantic vision of a Western ranch drew this family to a pasture on the Eagle River in the Rocky Mountains. Architect Duane Piper imagined a compound of buildings sitting low on the cusp of the river; it would be a postcard of horses, split-rail fences, meandering rooflines, and the mountains beyond. The cornerstone of the project would be a humble cabin intended to appear as genuine settler's quarters. The rest of the project would take its cues from the rambling, appended farmhouses of the West.

Authentic Colorado cabins characteristically use small logs, the round corners traditionally axed down and dovetailed.

The annexed buildings of the compound are a happy amalgam of board and batten, reclaimed barn wood with aged red paint remaining, and Telluride Gold stacked stone.

Fortuitously, the builder scavenged a load of beetle kill logs laying in a log yard down the river from the site. In what was called "Log Lab 101" the team, owner included, took traditional tools: foot adze, American and English broadaxe, draw knife, etc., and hacked the logs until they achieved the desired look. The cabin is the jewel on this property. It is only 1,000 square feet and is a self-sufficient compendium offering just enough room for a family of four. Slifer Designs took a very basic cabin and through discerning choices in furnishings concocted a peaceful haven that any cowpoke could appreciate.

ABOVE A cowboy theme is fitting for the main room in this cabin where vibrant Navajo rugs and patterns play well with denim.

OPPOSITE TOP This bedroom was made warm and serene by the selection of the falling feather fabric on a maize background.

OPPOSITE BOTTOM After a day of riding horses ant the ranch, what better place than this vintage tub to take a soak.

MOOSE ISLAND GETAWAY
NEW YORK

ARCHITECT, BUILDER, AND INTERIOR DESIGN: **PETER AND KIM HOLDERIED**

It took five years to complete this intimate camp on Moose Island, part of a chain of tiny islands on Lake Placid in the Adirondack Mountains. The island is thick with growth of cedar and birch, the camp is settled into its serene habitat and is adjacent to land designated "Forever Wild" by the State of New York. It was designed and built as a labor of love by one man and furnished by his talented wife. Three generations of the Holderied family spend time here in the summer. The family is of German/Bavarian descent and influences from these mountain regions are easily detected. No long design process was needed—in fact they sketched, submitted, and had the plan approved in quick order. The couple drew from their own pasts

and built a familiar form: a chalet with deep overhangs. It is replete with vintage touches and rustic finishes.

The house is conventionally framed, with log trusses supporting the floor boards and roof. The logs from nearby Willsboro were kept in perspective to the parcel, 8- and 12-inch diameters so not to overwhelm the site. They arrived green and with bark on them. Holderied single-handedly peeled, dried, and installed every log by himself, with the exception of the large interior middle beam that runs the length of the cabin. It took him an entire summer to build the fireplace, driving his truck down to a mainland river and returning with truckload after truckload of stone, loading it on a boat and up to the camp to be set.

OPPOSITE The Alpine cabin sits on an island and faces a tranquil strait. Building on an island can be a logistical challenge; great effort was made to use materials at hand or at the very least local. The larger logs were brought in from off-island, smaller branches and twigs for garnish were harvested from the site and employed as railings and gable screens.

LEFT Kim's artistic sense is evident in the furnishing of this camp. As was de rigueur in the camps at the turn of the century, souvenirs were showcased as the owner's trophies. There are a numerous artifacts from her travels that set the tone here. Antiquing is a sport for Kim, she combed the West for Navajo rugs, beaded articles of clothing, and pieces with just the right amount of age and character. They are artfully arranged and convey a decidedly Western emphasis to this Northeastern camp.

ABOVE Double doors open out to a balcony that over-looks the lake. The master bedroom has a romantic, campy feel that is ageless.

OPPOSITE BOTTOM A textural answer to a normally glossy room. To achieve this striking relief in the shower, Holderied put up green board used on bathroom walls and cut the river rock in half. He then anchored it with mortar and added a sunflower showerhead; he has created the illusion of showering in a natural waterfall.

OPPOSITE TOP The pioneer spirit reveals itself in the lighting: the twin chandeliers are made from old wagon wheels, and the hanging lights over the dining table are kerosene lamps that have been electrified. Kim's collection of well-aged vintage Beacon blankets and deer skins add a soft edge to the all-wood interior.

HUNTERS HAVEN
NORTH CAROLINA

NO ARCHITECT OR BUILDER INFORMATION IS AVAILABLE.

This quintessential Carolina mountain cabin was built in the early 1920s on a rolling grassy hill near Hurricane Lake and has been owned by the same family since 1940. Used as a hunting and fishing retreat, it became the springboard and inspiration for many homes in the Cashiers, North Carolina area. It is a summer cabin that is reclaimed from nature every spring—the doors are flung open, the winter residue is swept out, and another season begins.

By and large Mountain Top has been left to the elements to leave their mark. The cedar shake roof is thick with moss and sprouts of tree saplings. In this non-tropical rainforest it is impossible to keep the roof dry, so nature has been allowed to take its course.

The interior is authentic and unpretentious; the rugged texture of the finishes is offset by a cheery floral chintz covering the sofas. In a singularly simple space one room holds a gathering area, dining room, and sleeping loft. The loft in the front of the great room is accessed by playful "Indian doors" and rigged so that the ladder is hauled up once the "Indians" are upstairs.

Board and batten siding has been weathered and discolored in a variegated pattern of grays and browns and the long rooflines have grown verdant with moss—it is a charming sight.

ABOVE The great room at Mountain Top remains unchanged since the 1940s. The sandstone fireplace is the focal point, the boulders were reportedly transported here by mules. Over the mantel inspiring words from Shakespeare "and this our life, free from the haunts of men, finds sermons in stones; books in running brooks; and good in everything." In a forest of oak this species was used as trim for windows. The walls are Douglas fir with the golden patina only time can bestow. The beams are wormy chestnut, a wood no longer available unless reclaimed.

BELOW Mountain Top's primitive but efficient kitchen where over the years hunters and fishermen have prepared the catch of the day.

A TINY OASIS
NEW YORK

ARCHITECT: SHOPE RENO WHARTON ASSOCIATES
INTERIOR DESIGN: ALLAN SHOPE

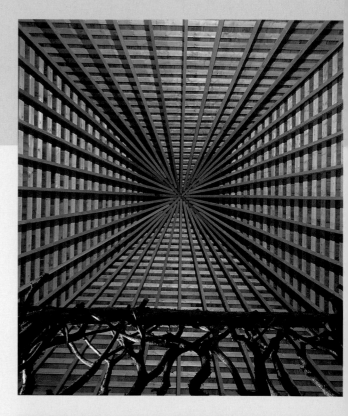

It is unimaginable that this diminutive structure could pack so much punch into 600 square feet. This is validation that solid design doesn't require a large bank account or excessive per-square-foot allowance to possess character and raw beauty.

Architect Allan Shope and his family needed a sanctuary, not an extravaganza, and this curiosity in the woods became a family project. Shope, an architect of remarkable homes, wanted for himself an unremarkable place—on the exterior. He chose to play his game of architectural subterfuge on a bucolic piece of land in upstate New York. On approach, the exterior "feels like nothing"—a compressed building, maybe an outbuilding. Upon entry the space explodes and there is a sense of being released. The feeling of surprise is overwhelming.

Much of the house was built by the Shopes themselves, with the exception of the stonework (the rock was pulled from the hillside behind the building and a mason was called in to complete the work). The materials list was limited to three items gathered from the site: 24-inch-wide white pine planks for flooring, cedar stick for decorative posts and railings, and hemlock for rafters.

OPPOSITE LEFT This mighty little home is, unbelievably, a weekend retreat for a family of six. The architect owner was taken with the comfortable, informal, and unique aspect of the Adirondack style and incorporated the best of it in this gem. The steep roof creates a hood that conceals the ethereal space that lies within. Cedar logs delineate the front veranda and expand the living space for this one-room wonder.
© 2003 Durston Saylor

LEFT AND DETAIL An astonishing room, the only room. There is a forced perspective created by the convergence of rafters at the ceiling peak. The amplified height makes the space appear grand. (A small kitchenette is positioned at the back of the building and sleeping quarters are accommodated in a loft space above the staircase.)
© 2003 Durston Saylor

OPPPOSITE BOTTOM RIGHT This is a simple yet complicated and visceral space. Stone and twig merge in a powerful sculpture that is the fireplace. Granite slabs are framed in aromatic cedar woven by Allan Shope. The spare lines of Stickley furniture allow the room to command attention here.
© 2003 Durston Saylor

RUSTIC HERE AND NOW

Contemporary rustic design is a function of the desire to explore new ways to bring the outside in, or to experiment with a fresh treatment of nature. Today's architects working in this arena have adopted the basic principles of contemporary design and then adapted them to a rustic format. Always looking to go out on a limb, these innovators design homes that are avant-garde and unique to their particular locale, putting their stamp on the rustic landscape. Here is a selection of contemporary rustic homes from the East and West.

This house features a hybrid of exterior finishes. Telluride Gold stone laid in dry-stacked manner is juxtaposed next to local spruce cut from dead standing forests. Copper is used throughout as the unifying thread; a patina process was applied to the metal to promote weathering. Due to the purity and dryness of the mountain air, exposed copper tends to turn brown or black rather than the verdigris shades more common in damp climates.

Photograph by Ryan A. Wolffe, Shepherd Resources, Inc.

RESORT RUSTIC
COLORADO

ARCHITECT: SHEPHERD RESOURCES, INC./ AIA, DOUGLAS M. DeCHANT, AIA, ADAM H. HARRISON
BUILDER: GEORGE SCHAEFFER CONSTRUCTION CO.   INTERIOR DESIGN: DESIGN PROJECTS INC., CHRISTINE STEVENS

The typical dilemma in resort architecture is that of space consideration, in this case very private clients building in a not very private location—a site with stunning mountain views on the slopes of Beaver Creek Ski resort in Colorado. The architect resolved the conflict by situating the house on the lower side of an embankment, bestowing it with a strong indoor/outdoor orientation. The well-informed and decisive clients wanted a modern mountain house with a slight English influence. They were looking for a mix of rustic and modern materials to distinguish the home from more literal mountain interpretations. What emerged from the drawing board was a simple yet dynamic modern home attired in mountain clothes.

The building was conceived as a collection of basic, rectangular building forms with gabled roofs. The central axis was envisioned as an old stone barn structure to which the other elements (garage, master suite, living room, and kitchen area) were attached. The home is an outside-in merging of stone, timber, and copper. Architect Douglas M. DeChant is a champion of this metal and often includes it in the repertoire of materials for the homes he designs. Here the roof is made of interlocking copper shingles, the conservatory is sheathed in copper, and light fixtures are fabricated of this earthy metal. It is a material rarely used in the East but has been much appropriated in the contemporary architecture of the New West.

The interior is crisp and concise in appearance, a clean combination of timber, glass, and stone set off by integral color veneer plaster. To promote the seamless transition between outside and in, massive commercial storefront windows were installed by grouting them directly into the stonework. In deference to the choice of form and material specification, the house has a sense of permanence and indestructibility.

Light is conveyed from the skylight to the core of the atrium, which is a backdrop for artwork from the owner's collection. Pieces are rotated throughout the year. This wall sculpture was a gift from an accomplished friend. Guardrails are fabricated from tempered sheet glass anchored by natural iron elements.

OPPOSITE A corridor of tree-like timbers reaches to a ridge skylight to form the framework for the central axis through the stone barn portion of the building. Glass and iron railings provide an industrial punctuation to the mountain dialect. Colored buff sandstone and distressed white oak floors define living areas and create a patchwork. These materials are rugged and require minimal care.

ABOVE The kitchen was arranged for a serious chef and provides ample work surfaces and professional appliances in a warm mix of old world and up-to-the-minute. The restful conservatory beyond the kitchen doubles as a sitting area and greenhouse.

RIGHT A New Age rustic powder room features a sandstone slab countertop, hammered copper lavatory, and mercury stained mirror.

The rooflines of this mountain retreat are overstated and run nearly to the ground, their pitches are calibrated at 30 degrees and form an irregular line that echoes the silhouette of the mountain ridge behind them. Depending on the time of day or year the house recedes into the scenery and the eye travels beyond it to the Green Mountains.

One of the design gauntlets of this project was to have the flues from five fireplaces within the house exit the building in one chimney. They needed to be twisted through channels and arches and brought up through this single, massive chimney.

VERMONT VERNACULAR
VERMONT

ARCHITECT: SELLERS AND COMPANY, DAVE SELLERS   BUILDER: HOOVER AUSTIN

Dave Sellers is an iconoclast in his approach to architecture. His office operates as an unconventional laboratory; an idea factory from which a supersonic molded plastic sled could be issued just as easily as an architectural plan. His renditions of rustic do not chase the Great Camp ethic but are a response to the local materials and his dedication to permanence and sustainability. A responsibility and deep respect for the land are inherent in his design doctrine, and in each commission he reaches for an environmentally sound way to use local resources—whether recycled or newly acquired—while resolving the particular requirements of each project.

For this commission the onus was on the architect to accommodate a large extended family and teens with a wide circle of friends. The house can sleep fifty if needed. Because of the high level of wear and tear, the materials needed to be user friendly and immutable. The team was blessed with an exquisite site in the Green Mountains of Vermont that offered broad mountain ridge views. In its previous incarnation the property was a maple sugar grove with hundreds of ancient maple trees and an old sugarhouse sited at the edge of the grounds. The footprint of the house was to be planted on the rock ledge that is prevalent in this region. All of these qualities were factored in to the equation. Sellers saw the opportunity to design a new structure that would re-create what had previously been on this land, and conceived a contemporary mountain house that emulates, in architectural terms, the landscape it occupies. The sugar maples were cut and used as interior structural columns, creating a grove within the home. Rocks that were blasted to clear space for the foundation were brought inside and used to shape the fireplace. The architect sought to mimic the zigzag of the ridge, drawing an irregular roofline that, when covered with snow, becomes part of the terrain. In essence the house merges with the landscape and appears to spring from the ground.

Integration was the mandate from the outset. The "windows" are not conventionally framed but are sheets of glass fit directly into the log framing. These portals become a wide aperture to take in the view. Doors, doorbells, and light fixtures are worked into the natural materials that have become the structure, creating a seamless transition between technology and nature.

The great room of the Sugar House showcases custom and site-specific furniture collaboratively designed by the architect and craftsmen Beeken/Parsons, a talented duo known for their clever fashioning of harvested "character wood." The dining area is the soul of this house and called for a durable and commodious table, fabricated from honey locust. Beeken/Parsons introduced leather to the chairs, using thick, wet leather that could be molded

for comfort. The leather was suspended over rock maple frames and fastened with an interesting lacing system.

Vermont bedrock pulled from the site was made into the fireplace and, true to Sellers' creed, not one stone or rock was imported. A change in ceiling height delineates the dining area and is set off by a perimeter of rope lights; the pendants over the dining table are made from hollowed burls.

The massive sugar maple trees taken from the site were installed in parallel rows, 10' to 16' apart. The beams were cut as 6 x 12s with three sides squared, and the remaining fourth side with bark on (or "wild" as the design team refers to it). The trees were set, then beam pockets sawn in and as beams, joists, and stairways were dovetailed together a grid pattern of trees and beams was formed, thus bracing the house. Names have been carved into these trees as the diary of a family is written.

One of Sellers' trademarks is the custom door and all of the doors were tailor-made for this house. Here, the front door is the singular Craftsman style detail in the home.

161

RIGHT Kitchen cabinets feature bark inlay and the contrast of black granite counters against the pale maple cabinets is stunning. The ceiling joists are slabs of wood with the wild edge turned on end, creating an undulating pattern overhead. Pendant lights are fashioned from turned maple burls with holes punched allowing them to breathe and shed light. These have become a signature of the architect, who is committed to using only home-specific lighting. Bar stools echo the use of leather in the dining chairs and have the added element of deer antler as fasteners.

OPPOSITE TOP A whimsical birch bed becomes a nest in this primordial guest bedroom. The rustic homes in Vermont have a lean look, not overly decorated; a log cabin playhouse and taxidermy duck are the sole ornaments in this room. Note the comical bedside "sconces" of sculpted maple burls mounted on copper tube arms.

OPPOSITE BOTTOM LEFT Sled benches woven from branches found on the property flank the front door.

OPPOSITE BOTTOM RIGHT The capacious mudroom accommodates equipment for many and for at least ten sports. A mural of Sugarbush Mountain Ski Resort inspires skiers to take a day on the slopes.

EAST MEETS WEST IN UPSTATE NEW YORK

NEW YORK

DESIGNER: **Neal and Sweet Studio Designs, Jonathan Sweet**
STRUCTURAL ENGINEER: **Steve Smith, P.E.**
BUILDER: **Landmark Builders, Neal and Sweet**

This log home in upstate New York on the edge of the Adirondack Park is pure hybrid. The main portion of the house was built in the 1980s and a sizable one-room wing was affixed in recent years. The owners were enchanted with the ranches of the West and engaged designer Jonathan Sweet to meld western and Adirondack styles allowing him to author a new rustic vernacular. Known for his award-winning furniture designs, Sweet was given carte blanche on the new wing. He conceived the architecture, furniture, and lighting to illustrate his new rustic design doctrine merging the two Americas.

Departing from tradition, Sweet torqued proportion to a degree that the trusses form a surreal framework for the exotic furnishings. Surprisingly, these enormous logs, which measure up to 38" in diameter, came not from Canada or the West but from New York State.

His furniture pieces reflect Sweet's willingness to step out of the box: barn beams, stone, leather, and slate find a home together in unexpected liaisons with farm implements and other found objects.

The new great room wing was grafted on to an existing log structure nearly doubling the square footage of this home. Their affection for the West led them to import a herd of longhorn steer to the farm.

CENTER The striking floors are parquet, made of slabs cut from the end grain of barn timbers and installed as tiles yielding a cobblestone effect. In a gesture of outside-in, granite wainscot girdles the room; it was appropriated from the owner's quarry. All of the upholstered furniture was designed and built by Sweet. The black surface on the sofa is slate that has been run through the dishwasher, epoxyed on a frame, and glazed. The base of the dining table is an inverted D-8 bulldozer blade topped with glass. A chandelier over this table was made from a trolley used originally to move bales of hay. The wagon wheel game table light is outfitted in a hunting motif and tells the story of heading West: tepee style shades of ash veneer, decorated with horsehair tassels, pheasant feathers, and bullet cases—nothing is considered out of bounds for this designer.

BELOW Cabinets in the bar were an unlikely coupling of Western rodeo mixed with Japanese Victorian. Sweet prefers exotic woods for their character, Brazilian lacewood cabinets are accented with copper and are glazed with hand-rolled glass reclaimed from an old glove factory. The flooring here is leather tile, homage to Gloversville, New York's leather capital. Saddle bar stools are hitched up to a table topped with a redwood burl slab. A chandelier was rigged from a triple tree pulled from a horse-drawn wagon, the hammered steel shades are rendered in a longhorn motif.

A CONTEMPORARY ALPINE LODGE
COLORADO

ARCHITECT: SHEPHERD RESOURCES, INC./AIA - DOUGLAS M. DECHANT, AIA, MICHAEL J. BUCCHIN
BUILDER: BECK BUILDING COMPANY INTERIOR DESIGN: SLIFER DESIGNS: YVONNE JACOBS, KATHERINE PEEL

Many denizens of this part of the Rockies near Vail, Colorado, are of mid-European descent. They have brought with them a mountain architecture sensibility that hails from the Alps. This home was built on the slopes of a ski resort as a place of restoration for a family of Czech heritage. The architect, Douglas M. DeChant, listened carefully to the clients and the site and responded with this cutting-edge lodge, a new and sophisticated mountain-appropriate structure. This architect has no signature or sentimental ties to the past, he is developing a new architectural vocabulary that is pushing the edge of the rustic envelope.

For this house DeChant focused on the quality and movement of light and space. He sought to keep every room intimate and peaceful—no small feat in an 8500-square-foot house. Rich finishes, textures, and materials create a warm sanctuary for a family. The language is composed of strong organic materials, primarily rock, plaster, and wood with hints of stucco. The level of detail reveals itself in layers. The experience becomes a process of discovery, unfolding as one spends time in the house. The woodwork alone is remarkable, hand-chiseled beams intricately coped and joined were influenced by traditional timber expressions found in the mountain settings of northern Europe and Scandinavia.

Rather than create overt architecture, the team focused on designing a range of experiences for the site. They wanted each interior space to engage all the senses and lead to an associated outdoor experience as expressed in the outdoor terraces, decks, or balconies. The paths and passages are part of the odyssey.

OPPOSITE The overriding impression of this home is its tangible solidity. Squarely planted on substantial stone piers, it is a fortress that stands up to the powerful topography of the Rocky Mountains. Exterior building stone and massive landscape rocks were imported from Montana. The rocks are loosely set, projecting an image of strong yet less refined foundational elements. Interior and exterior materials relate; reclaimed Douglas fir was used for both. DeChant favors copper in his architecture; the roof chimneys are a woven copper scrim and copper-clad windows, copper panels, and preformed copper shingles skin portions of exterior walls. Consistency dictated the use of heavy-gauge slate for the roofing material.

LEFT In a command performance, the architect replicated, from the client's former home, this organic stair rail in the entry landing. The use of integral color veneer plaster is common in the contemporary homes of the West. It is a familiar treatment in northern Europe and is the touchstone for the interior finish of this house. The compound is tinted and applied over Sheetrock and at the cure point is hit with a wet brush for a softer look. Floors are wide-plank white oak from Europe. The stone floors are Colorado Buff sandstone.

OPPOSITE Reclaimed Douglas fir timbers frame the mountain vista beyond. The wood was salvaged from various locations, the Denver Ice House and Top Gun Air Force Base in Miramar, California, among them. They have been seasoned, hand planed, stained, and then rubbed with pumice to knock off the sheen and leave a milky residue.

Liberal use of the chamfer throughout the house is a craftsman detail, softening the many planes and angles of wood in this house, as seen in the beveled edge of the stair treads, the trusses, and the window frames.

ABOVE All of the cabinetry and woodwork is custom designed and bench built. It required a workforce of forty people to execute the elaborate finish work in this house. Each piece of wood, iron, slab stone, etc., was thoughtfully detailed and terminated. The interior designer settled on a bright, European country scheme for this family gathering place.

ABOVE Bunking Bavarian style. Leaping deer and loping moose animate the children's room at this Colorado chalet.

RIGHT An arched doorway provides an inviting passage to this intimate study. The wide plank reclaimed Douglas fir walls and subdued lighting make this room alluring for a roaring fire and a nap.

LEFT This clever sideboard was designed by the architect. It is a partner to the architecture of this room and serves as a spatial divider between the dining room and walkway. Upon scrutiny one can see that it's a marriage of many materials: reclaimed Douglas fir, mahogany, and natural iron.

RIGHT The story of the Red Peg: The complexity of the truss system and dexterity of the craftsmen led the owner to suggest that if one innocuous peg were pulled the entire house would collapse—a craftsman painted the peg red . . . and so the story goes.

FACE-LIFT FOR AN A-FRAME

VERMONT

ARCHITECT: SELLERS AND COMPANY, DAVE SELLERS BUILDER: NORTHLAND CONSTRUCTION, RUSS BENNETT

The headline for this house should read: Dark Doghouse-like 1970s Cabin Becomes Tranquil Mountain Retreat. By all accounts this architectural malady needed a prescription for a face-lift. The owners wanted to convert an antiquated hybrid A-frame into a viable family retreat. The word "renovation" trivializes the extensive changes that transformed this Vermont ski house into a compelling rustic home.

The site is a sylvan setting in the Green Mountains—the location made the home a keeper. The architect was asked to open it up and bring order to the various living areas. Rooflines were changed dramatically to increase the volume of the space and accommodate a master bedroom suite and children's rooms. The common spaces needed to be vastly expanded; critical to the project's success was the creation of flow and spatial-use patterns.

The builder and skilled arborist cleared and cleaned up the landscape so the occupants could embrace the outdoors rather than focus their orientation inward. The first order was to punch out the roof and add some architectural interest in the form of "swoopy" dormers, a term coined by architect Dave Sellers. The builder had ordered a v-groove pine board for the walls but what was delivered was a floor board that typically shows the reverse side grooved to prevent cupping. Fate served them well, by using the corduroyed side of the boards for decorative woodwork they created an unusual corrugated paneling that suited the décor.

Interiors are innovative: bedrooms have 3-D murals, one bathroom offers a boulder for a sink. Yet in keeping with the straightforward Vermont disposition, the few painted walls are a soft and mellow mustard and furnishings are spare.

At the close of the project the family had a triumph in this woodland treasure rendered in Vermont rustic vernacular.

LEFT AND DETAIL A hedgerow of maples greets upon entry. Seller's signature flared -foot tree trunks are sunk into collars of stone set in mortar. The contractor, seeking to make the setting for the trees more interesting, sent his workman down to the river with a bucket to fetch the rounded pebbles that were embedded into the concrete well.

Stained concrete floors were deemed appropriate, both for wear and for a radiant heat source to be used at the core of the house.

OPPOSITE This mountain lodge in the Mad River Valley in Vermont, underwent a metamorphosis and became a light-filled, pleasantly rusticated refuge for a family. From a small dark cabin emerged this enchanting ski house with three-story mountain views. Hyperbolic windows fused to the structure grant the facade a wide-eyed look.

Two slabs of cherry were fused with butterfly joints to become the dining table. This was designed by Sellers as a nod to the great furniture craftsman George Nakashima. An ark-like, fanciful chandelier was made of hand-blown glass and Plexiglas.

ABOVE The team went all out on the kitchen in deference to the wife who is as much a culinary artist as an avid skier. The cabinets are elaborate and sleek in a rustic way and were built out of maple with birch bark recessed panels that are vaguely arrowhead in shape. Vermont soapstone forms the sinks and countertops and was deemed a logical choice for this house.

LEFT A hollowed out marble boulder set on twin pedestals became the powder room sink, a "primitive" solution for this rustic retreat.

HIGH-TECH RUSTIC IN THE NEW WEST
COLORADO

ARCHITECTS: **CCY ARCHITECTS** BUILDER: **GEORGE SHAEFFER CONSTRUCTION CO.**
LANDSCAPE: **LAND DESIGN BY ELLISON** INTERIOR DESIGN: **DESIGN COALITION, DAVID KRAJESKI**

Progressive architecture has found a home in the Rockies. The firm CCY is known for its innovative adaptation of regional architecture and use of traditional elements with a contemporary viewpoint. They are masters of the hybrid home that is fast becoming part of the mountain idiom in Western landscapes. This sleek house represents the architecture of the New West in form and function. It has been outfitted with state-of-the-art technology featuring touch screen panel controls in each room regulating lighting, music, video, temperature, security, and window shades. Modernity set aside, Wildwood appears to be a chiseled version of an ancient stone ledge and the source of the stream that flows from beneath it. It is accessed from a winding road in Colorado's Rockies. The sloping site has long-range western mountain views unobstructed by trees.

The owner was taken with the concept of a log home but wanted a more sophisticated interpretation. Although the house is 10,000 square feet, the scale was minimized by breaking up the mass into simple volumes. Architects John Cottle, Chris Touchette, and Todd Kennedy took a deconstructive approach and rendered the home as a series of log cabins with glazed (glass) areas acting as the connective tissue, enabling the occupants to be in touch with the surrounding environment. In doing so they fulfilled the client's desire for an interactive experience between the landscape and interiors.

The sturdy cabins have been executed in stacked square log construction (log masonry), laid up in 12" courses with teak relief coursing every 48" on the interior walls. The material used was reclaimed Douglas fir, the majority of which came from dismantled lumber and paper mills in Oregon. This horizontal feature is reflected in the facing walls of stacked Telluride Gold stone, the masonry banding rendered in inverted stone parquetry. This motif continues as a decorative girdle on the exterior (where the strapping is larger fir) giving the effect that the buildings are part of a Jacob's ladder held together by lacing—no mortar or chinking, only gravity.

In contrast to the solid use of these traditional earthy materials are the contemporary and refined finishes of the windows and doors interpreted in African mahogany. The cabinets throughout are sleek and were a collaboration between the architect, interior designer, and furniture maker. Asian allusions and subtle boundaries between interior and exterior spaces create a meditative quality in this home. A soothing natural color palette is brought to life through textural contrasts of fabrics and accessories.

OPPOSITE Each area of the grounds has a distinct character. Plantings along the water feature and at the entry are more detailed and lush, and thin out to a more arid zone blending with the existing scrub. A grassy lawn takes its contours from the rectilinear nature of the architecture. The shape of the house created a courtyard that was developed as a garden in a meditative space. Many of the plantings on this property are native species.

© Robert Millman Photography

ABOVE The stunning landscape architecture was beautifully articulated by Glen Ellison and Pam Granade. To further marry the buildings to the site, stone ledges were conceived to cascade from the house and reach out to the landscape. These large blocks of Telluride Gold carry through the site, in the terraces, driveway, and pool areas. There are three water features on this property; all are operational year-round.

The buildings are unified not only by composition of spaces but by layering of textures. Copper roofs offset the vigorous pattern of shake roofs in a pleasant interplay of material and surfaces. The standing seam copper oxidizes to a dark brown color; it is low maintenance and long lasting.

© Robert Millman Photography

ABOVE A Telluride Gold stone stacked fireplace is the centerpiece of the great room. Antique oak flooring with a unique sawn face was garnered from old barns in the eastern United States. The oak abuts a Colorado Buff sandstone floor—precisely coped to fit.
A muted color scheme in neutrals and browns allows the art collection and landscape to speak, conferring a peaceful aura to the home and the furnishings.

OPPOSITE TOP LEFT A modern rustic composition as seen in the powder room. Fully integrated plaster walls are the staging for a vanity that appears to be suspended in air.

OPPOSITE TOP RIGHT A hallway wall illustrates the positive/negative space banding that wraps the

building. The emphasis is on craftsmanship and detail, most evident in the stacked timber finger-joined corner detail executed like a fine piece of cabinetry. The compound was designed to accommodate specific pieces from the owner's vast art collection.

OPPOSITE BOTTOM LEFT A color palette of saffron and cinnamon was painted in the guest cabin. The bed is dressed in silk and imparts a contemporary Asian spirit to the room.

OPPOSITE BOTTOM RIGHT The flooring material in the stairway was salvaged from an abandoned teak warehouse in Burma. The newel posts, designed by the architect, are all carved from a single beam that measured 5' square by 120' long.

THE NEXT STEP

It is an architectural paradox that modern can't be rustic at the same time. As architecture writer Joseph Giovanni says, "Architecture has negotiated the relationship between man and nature since the cave. But in the 20th century, when the machine invaded the garden in the form of hard-edged buildings, an intangible seam divided the modernist house from nature, and the eye could never quite make the two whole again . . . . An architect could be modern or traditional: it was an either/or choice."

The common perception is that modern translates it to angular forms—sleek, polished surfaces that are the antithesis of rustic. This is changing. Mavericks of modern design, architects and scholars known for their abstracted urban and suburban structures, are being commissioned to design homes that work their modern aesthetic into a woodland context. These futuristic abodes become intellectual endeavors for their creators. They have reconciled the two worlds by viewing nature for its sculptural possibilities, and are designing homes that will become one with the land and the landscape and not simply occupy it.

In the spirit of Frank Lloyd Wright, the architects of today and tomorrow are able to deliver a fully integrated home by creating site-specific everything for these unusual spaces. Technology is the new craft and it will dictate some of the finer points of design. I believe as our realities become more complex we, as consumers, will demand that our environments become simplified.

As is the case with anything avant-garde, the more exposure to the public, the easier it is to digest. These New Age homes are getting a lot of press, creating novel definitions of this style, and laying the groundwork for a new generation of rusticators.

NEW AGE RUSTIC
COLORADO

ARCHITECT: **RKD Architects Inc., Jack Snow, Sally Brainerd**
BUILDER: **RKD Architects Inc.**

A dramatic site was addressed with a striking architectural reply in this surreal composition. Looking to break out of the mold of traditional mountain and resort architecture, architect Jack Snow cast off archetypal forms and rethought the process. Striving for a complete interface with nature, he studied the topography of the site, a 70-acre parcel in the Rocky Mountains with canyon walls, springs, and creek beds, and saw the possibility for something organic and sculptural. Water and stone are the commanding features of the site, hence the name Waterstone.

A stone tower is the axis for the project; from this stems a series of living "pods" (modules) that are linked by glass bridges that straddle the streams below. The well-orchestrated arrangement combines curved, angled, and sloped forms suggesting either a museum-quality model or a space station. This is the now and future of rustic—retaining the indigeny and geology of the site while becoming part of it and embracing a bold design vocabulary of the 21st century.

Waterstone embodies the concept of a "vertical" home where the design is completely site specific, the architecture is fused to landscape, and all interior finishes and furnishings are bespoke and tailored to the occupants and their habitat. The repertoire of materials is limited to steel, patinated copper, quarry-marked sandstone, slate, beech, and cedar. Spaces may be linear and abstract but they remain intimate.

This futuristic home is perfectly situated in the crease between two rock-strewn canyon walls. The three irregular pods are built of angular massive stone forms with sloped copper cylinders cantilevered over the landscape. Timber beams intersect these contours and support a corrugated, weathered steel roof. The overall effect is extraordinary.
Photograph by Ron Ruscio Photography

LEFT Stacked geometric shapes counterbalance each other creating a seesaw of stone, timber, and metal. This courtyard is the guest-pod access area. The entry to this house is progressive—arriving on a circular driveway, crossing a brook, and ending in this courtyard where the lower-level entrance to the house draws one up a stairway to the living spaces. The exterior materials and forms, such as this steel railing, are repeated inside.
Photograph courtesy RKD

BELOW A tranquil waterfall slides down the slate and stone walls to a pool in the lower-level entry at Waterstone. Consideration was taken for light from above a designated art wall and the desire to draw people up the stairway to the main level on the second floor. In a house of stone, the architect wanted to introduce a lighter element and designed the floating stairway using steel framing and wood treads.
Photograph by Ron Ruscio Photography

ABOVE Rectilinear glass bridges and curved lookouts allow the occupants to be engaged in the scenery. This kitchen slopes out over a pond; the repetitive rick rack of the corrugated steel forms a pleasing fringe for the roofline.

OPPOSITE A slate fireplace in tandem with stone and copper walls creates drama in this intimate dining space.
©2005/Eclipse Photography/Billy Doran/eclipsephoto.org

THE FUTURE OF RUSTIC

ARCHITECT: **RKD ARCHITECTS**

RKD Architects in Edwards, Colorado, have hypothesized what the dynamic rustic home of the future will be and have envisioned a string of pods connected by bridges to prove their point. The pods open up the spaces. Rather than have large interior expanses, more exterior walls will allow for more glass. Additionally the clear corridors linking the pods keep the occupant in touch with the outside by becoming living spaces. This home is strung out parallel to the view. The glass walls vanish—you are in the landscape.

Aside from obvious advances like the "smart house" and geothermal heating systems, new technology has lifted constraints—the computer is able to work out calculations for out-of-the-ordinary building specifications and all the curves that nature can throw to insure a well-engineered house. Future craftsmen will use these calculations to take rustic design to the next level.

If one were to take the current condition of contemporary rustic and extrapolate what it might look like in the future, the direction seems to be less is more. More glass and less structure permit the natural surroundings to take center stage. The distinctions between out and in will become imperceptible. The usual suspects—stone, log, and branch—will be joined by an increased use of weathered metals and other components that are altered by the elements and communicate an earthy feel. Perhaps indigenous will take a backseat to ingenuity, and composites blending natural and technologically advanced materials will become not only acceptable but desirable. Or, in an idealogical U-turn, all that is revered in the rustic philosophy will be upended by the use of man-made substances posing as nature: a clear acrylic deer head, a multicolored resin tree branch, and so forth, opening up a brave new world of rustic simulacra, a plastic universe parallel to the organic one.

Stripped-down décor and minimalist interiors will focus the orientation outdoors. Simplicity will be of utmost importance, site-specific furniture in the form of built-ins will be the order. I predict ultra-textured fabrics will be on the drawing boards to fill a current gap in textile offerings.

Architect Jack Snow's rendering of a futuristic rustic home.
RKD Architects

This intimate room, designated for playing cards and board games, is a blueprint for rustic decoration. The architect specified nickel-spaced planks for the walls throughout this Adirondack camp. The walls were painted deep green and the floors are reclaimed chestnut covered with a Tibetan folk rug. Designer Ann Stillman O'Leary chose a quilted deer medallion fabric for the sofa, which has been cloaked in a deer skin. Antiques in the form of authentic 19th century oil paintings, a Gustav Stickley leather top game table, and a French elm coffee table provide some history. The sleeping porch beyond sports a woodland bed of mosaic twig and bark. Peter Pennoyer Architects, Cascade Builders.

DECORATION: THE LATEST AND GREATEST IN RUSTIC DÉCOR

It's true that if the bones of a house are good everything looks better, but if the furnishings are poorly chosen, the desired effect can fall flat. The décor is where the eye stops and where the first impression is made. Dare to be different but not Disney. In rustic interiors it is tempting to over-twig, over-theme, and overwhelm the senses. When in doubt avoid cliché and defer to simplicity and restraint; it will outclass excess. This chapter is a "how to" guide to the successful rustic interior for cabin, camp, and lodge; a veritable tip sheet on furniture, lighting, metalwork, fabrics, and accessories that will create the desired effect for the rustic home.

RUSTIC INTERIORS

Comfort is the common denominator when furnishing the rustic home. Most of the houses featured in this book are vacation homes and the owners are looking to escape the constraints of their everyday life, lift their spirits, and recharge their batteries. They achieve this through varying degrees of comfort and informality in their furniture and accessories. Many choose to emphasize the whimsical potential inherent in the use of natural forms, others strive for simplicity and asceticism.

In many cases, what was considered cutting edge in 1989 is considered trite now. Much like the country trend of the early 1980s, maturity leads to sophistication. We've come a long way from cow figurines. At the dawn of the rustic renaissance, décor tended toward the obvious, heavy-handed, literal symbols of the outdoors. Today there is a new level of artistry and finesse—the ubiquitous moose silhouette replaced now by a series of framed antique hand-colored moose bookplates perhaps. As tastes become more discerning a more refined array of furnishings will be introduced to the market.

A guest bedroom at Camp Birch Point exemplifies the benefit of using antiques to create personality when going for a vintage look. All the doors and door hardware were picked from salvage yards; the beds are antique hickory and woven splint from the Old Hickory Furniture Company; and other appointments, such as the electrified kerosene lamps and accent table, represents the fruits of years of scouring antique markets.

The well-furnished rustic home shouldn't be blatantly rustic head to toe, nor should it be "decorator-y." In researching this book my biggest obstacle came in finding homes that got it right. Nothing is less inspiring than a room in which every piece of décor is identifiable by a manufacturer; it shows lack of creativity and confidence and worst of all apathy. A truckload of new furniture delivered on Tuesday does not exude character or warmth.

The best of traditional rustic décor is an amalgam of the new (generally upholstery or lighting), old treasures that don't have to be rustic but have personality and patina, and a few genuine one-of-a-kind rustic pieces. The home should reflect the personality of the owners and be a showcase for their hobbies and collections, whether it stars a series of vintage postcards depicting the National Parks or carved antler buttons.

There is no prototype for a traditional rustic great room but texture is always a key element.

A prescription for a handsome display would be: an antique tufted pile rug in deep but timeworn coloration; a piece or two of leather upholstery (preferably distressed and with antique nail heads). Other upholstered pieces might include nubby chenille, a tapestry fabric featuring a flora or fauna motif, a piece with antler or horn decoration, and faux or real fur accents. Antique tables and occasional pieces will elevate the character of the room as will at least one well-designed piece inspired by nature, a mosaic twig table for example.

The modern rustic home is a different story. Minimal furnishings designed specifically for the spaces (site-specific furniture) seem to work best for these homes. The pieces should have simple lines—not to detract from nature beyond—but the textures are likely to be complex.

The categories of decoration that help tell the rustic story are furniture from out of the woods, lighting, metalwork, antler, and wall décor, and the plethora of soft goods used to accessorize a home.

ABOVE In deference to the gracious homes of the past, a private niche for telephone conversation was carved out. The "telephone nook" at Lean-To Camp doubles as a space for fly-fishing equipment. Tramp art is at home in rustic environs; the knobby, zigzag carvings and tobacco brown play well as accent pieces such as this eccentric little chair.

LEFT A well-appointed vignette at Forever Wild camp in Keene Valley, New York. The table lamp and birch frame are from Rusted Rock Studio and Gallery.

Photograph by Mark Hobson

FURNITURE

The rustic home deserves a couple of special pieces of furniture created from nature. In the last few years the better authentic rustic antiques have been snapped up by savvy collectors. Because this genre occupies a small niche in the antique world, good pieces are currently hard to come by and when they do, the bidding is high.

There are a handful of very talented new rustic furniture makers across the country. Their work is much sought after and, in recent years, their commissions have commanded top dollar. There are two primary venues for these artisans and up-and-comers to show their wares: at the Western Design Conference in Cody, Wyoming, and at the Rustic Furniture Makers Fair at the Adirondack Museum in Blue Mountain Lake, New York. These are good places for homeowners to get a primer on the art of rustic furniture.

Stick Furniture

From the crudest four leg, slab-top table to an elaborate and graceful chair, stick and twig furniture are lighthearted enhancements for any room. These are generally small pieces—tables and chairs—made from branches and sprigs with bark on that are strapped, nailed, or mortised together. The zip code determines the species: in the East yellow birch and cedar are the usual suspects, Southerners seek out locust, willow, and laurel, the Midwest is known for hickory and willow, and in the West they prefer peeled pole to real twig work.

Hickory furniture is a subcategory of stick that has enjoyed a rebirth in the last 15 years coinciding with the rustic movement. It is manufactured by a number of companies from the tight hard saplings of the hickory tree and comes predominantly from Indiana, where for the last 125 years the Old Hickory Furniture Company has produced container loads of their sturdy wares. Seats are woven splint, wicker, or upholstered.

RIGHT From the West, Doug Tedrow of Wood River Rustics delivers well-designed and executed mosaic case goods. This impressive cabinet is titled *Up at Dawn*, a comment on the sunburst pattern that adorns the front of the piece as well as its 9' height. The boxes are alder, logs are lodgepole pine, and the mosaic work is willow. Details are important: the pegs are antler, the lashings are rawhide, and the pulls are clay with a turquoise glaze. Leather fringed cow horns can be used as vases or candle holders. This piece won an award for excellence at the Western Design Conference in 2004.
Photograph courtesy Doug Tedrow

BELOW This is one of a collection of Memory Chairs created by Dan Mack. It combines found objects with the natural form chair frame, and alludes to the interplay of man with nature by fusing cultural artifacts with trees. Mack believes that chairs are for more than sitting; they are part of the story of life, they witness events, they become part of the memory and family history.

Photograph by Adam Kurtz

OPPOSITE A tête-à-tête rendered in willow shoots by Bill Perkins of Sleeping Bear Twig Furniture in Michigan. His work reflects such diverse influences as the Art Nouveau movement, Wiener Werkstatte, and fellow rusticator Clifton Monteith.

Photograph courtesy Bill Perkins

ABOVE Cottage-style dining at a Canadian camp. Hemlock boards were reclaimed from old local barns, milled, and reincarnated as floors and trim throughout the cottage. The furniture is from the Old Hickory Furniture Company in Indiana. The dining table is made of yellow birch.

Photograph by stacey brandford photography

Peeled Pole Furniture

The bark is removed from the branches, burls, and twigs for this furniture. The underlying wood is often stained and finished with wax. The more intricate, finer pieces are traditionally found in the East; in the West they favor heftier pieces of the tree, as well as burl and unusual species such as the twisted juniper or the straight-as-an-arrow lodgepole pine. There are a number of companies across the country manufacturing production pieces in simple straight uniform logs, basics like beds, dressers, and chairs for the customer not requiring a custom look.

In the West, Thomas Molesworth made a notable contribution to natural furnishings in the 1930s. Inspired by the Arts and Crafts movement he experimented with indigenous burl, leather, antler, and Indian and cowboy artifacts. His quest produced unrivaled and completely original cowboy-style furniture. His pieces are much sought after—new interpretations in the spirit of Molesworth are available from a handful of firms keeping the style alive.

OPPOSITE TOP A room vignette created by Midnight Farms showcases a mosaic twig console table with a root base.
Photograph courtesy Midnight Farms

RIGHT Inspired by Molesworth, The Great Camp Collection offers pieces that have become Western American classics. Here they've integrated a wool Native American weaving into the leather upholstery.

Photograph courtesy The Great Camp Collection

OPPOSITE BOTTOM LEFT Larry Hawkins of Hawkins Unique Rustic Mosaic Twig Art Furniture built and embellished this sideboard in the traditional mosaic manner.
Photograph courtesy Larry Hawkins

OPPOSITE RIGHT Intricate mosaic work and wildlife oil painting on this clock is the handiwork of Larry Hawkins.
Photograph courtesy Larry Hawkins

Mosaic Work Furniture

Mosaic work furniture features case goods that have half twigs arranged and tacked in ornate geometric patterns. The diversity of bark color and twig size in combination with the repetitive ribbed effect create appealing compositions.

Burl and Root Furniture

Maple, yellow birch, redwood, and lodgepole pine trees all tend to sprout growths or "inflammations" known as burls that when split and sliced make excellent tables and organic pieces. This often eccentric, free-form furniture plays up the asymmetry of burls and root formations and can be a sculptural addition to even an urban space.

LEFT Barney Bellinger of Sampson Bog Studio created this fly fisherman's cabinet (titled *Jumped Up)* from lodgepole pine burls, and pine bark veneer. It features a twig apron and a hidden drawer under the tabletop, which is 100-year- old curly oak. The pictorial of a leaping brook trout was painted by Bellinger, a fly fishing aficionado.
Photograph courtesy Sampson Bogs Studios

ABOVE This baroque yellow birch settee was created by man-of-the-woods Barry Gregson and his son Matthew. It has been outfitted with cherry burl drink-holders and bowls, a cherry burl, and a walnut and curly cherry seat.
Photograph courtesy Barry Gregson

Arts and Crafts Style Furniture

The Arts and Crafts movement at the beginning of the 20th century balked at mass production and the overwrought garish Victorian furniture of the time, advocating instead a return to simpler ideas, honest craftsmanship, and sturdy construction. Gustav and Leopold Stickley embraced the movement and built a furniture collection that is still in production today. The clean lines of these quarter-sawn white oak pieces, although not in and of themselves rustic, lend themselves to nearly any rustic room. The contours of the Mission style furniture have been replicated or interpreted by countless artisans in numerous woods and are widely available in the market.

East meets west in Soho. This chic, modern table was designed and built by Jonathan Sweet. The artist is reaching for a new rustic that fuses Eastern and Western materials and Craftsman concepts with a downtown attitude. It is the direction that rustic will take in the years to come, honest and well-conceived modern design expressed in rustic materials.

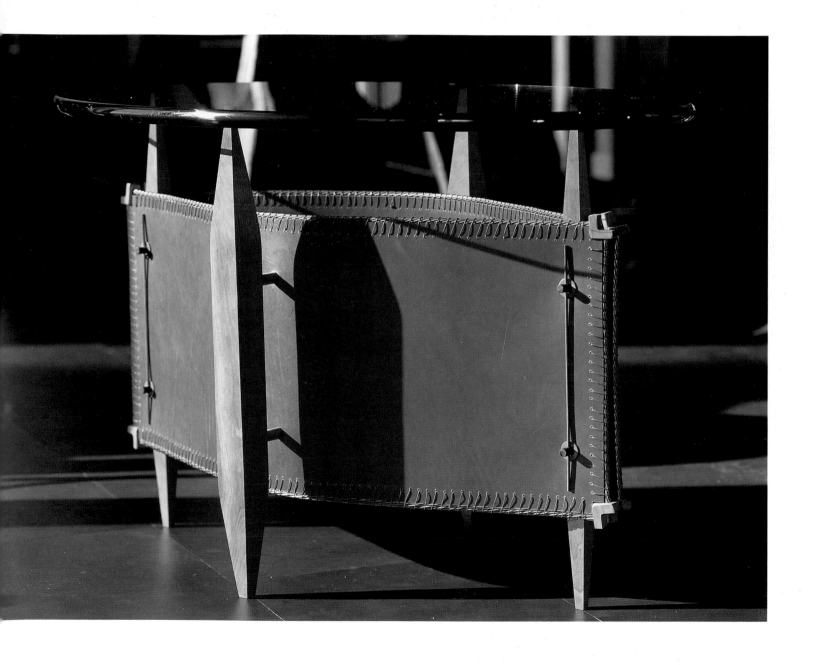

Carved Wood, Tramp Art, and Black Forest Furniture

Although these categories of furniture are not out of the woods they are rustic by association and subject matter and make excellent appointments to the rustic home.

John Bryan, one of the most accomplished wood-carvers in the East created this splendid mantelpiece. His refined bas-relief door panels and mantels are essays in sculpture and grace homes across the continent. This tasteful carving was commissioned by a fly fisherman and exquisitely details the gear of this gentleman's sport.
Photograph by Warren Roos

ABOVE Interior Designer Ann Stillman O'Leary rendered this rustic still life. Unable to locate the ideal tramp art mirror, she designed this piece with a framed camp scene under glass at the top. Mulligan and Phillips executed the intricate design by notching out strips of wood and layering them in the tramp art manner. The demilune table features a reclaimed barnboard top, undulating twig apron, and laurel base. It was designed by O'Leary and executed by Tiger Mountain Woodworks.
© Gary Hall Photography

LEFT Craftsman David Norton created the burned-wood panels for the doors, custom built by Howard Hatch. The trillium battens in this powder room are crafted of spalted maple, apple wood, cherry, walnut, pine, and fir—a skilled tribute to the local species.
Photograph by Cheryle St. Onge

RIGHT Peter Fillerup of Wild West Designs cast this striking bronze chandelier that tells the story of the migration of the Wapiti deer. Cream marbleized glass panels cast a warm glow on this dining room.
Photograph by Matt Turley Photographer

BELOW The Montana chandelier from Crystal Farm, 6' wide and made of fallow deer and elk antlers.
Photograph courtesy Crystal Farm

LIGHTING

This is one category of decoration that offers an abundance of innovative and well-designed pieces. Hammered wrought iron is available from individual forges as well as more mainstream manufacturers. Because it is hand wrought, custom requests and sizes are easily accommodated. The color and texture from the blows of the hammer make iron a suitable choice for the rustic home. Cast bronze is esteemed for the level of detail and virtual likeness to nature it can achieve. There are amazing fixtures that are bronze replications of branches or pinecones as well as those depicting 3-D wildlife scenes. Antlers abound and are mandatory in some permutation in the rustic home, usually in the form of a show-stopping chandelier or lamp. There are a number of well-respected antler craftspeople with the talent and know-how to elegantly integrate the bulbs and hide the wiring.

To rusticate a conventional lamp, shades add the finishing touch—rawhide, burlap, chamois, feather, bark, pressed paper with leaves. Lightbulbs shouldn't be overlooked as an important aspect in conveying the proper feel. An amber, flame-shaped bulb, used on a sconce, could be just the thing for setting the right mood in a dining room.

A sconce and a pendant light from Christopher Thomson, whose training as a potter is evident in his handling of molten metal.

Photographs by Peter Vitale

Lean-To Studio creates award winning rustic lighting (by any definition.) They incorporate real botanicals, bark, twig, pinecones, acorns, copper, mica and glass into their awe-inspiring compositions. The fern in this chandelier becomes visible when illuminated.

Photograph courtesy Lean-To Studio

ARTISAN AT WORK

JOAN BENSON AND STEPHEN KENT
Antler Artisans

High in the Rocky Mountains above the aspens, the pines, and the jagged peaks roam the mule deer and magnificent elk. Cowboys, hikers, and senior citizen groups gather antlers shed from these animals in the late summer and early fall. It's from these collections that Crystal Farm acquires the antlers to create their lighting and furniture. Stephen Kent and Joan Benson established this company in the early 1980s and have become the preeminent antler lighting and furniture purveyors in this country.

Only the highest-quality antlers are used by Crystal Farm in Redstone, Colorado. They are left in their natural state, the individual shapes allowed to play a large part in the design of each piece. Fallow deer antlers unavailable here are sourced from Europe and flown in to the studios. Stephen and Joan have drawn their inspiration from Western and European designs, their offerings run the gamut from a Western upholstered longhorn chaise to a Bavarian carved chandelier.

Joan Benson of Crystal Farm is drilling holes to allow for wiring and electrification of a spectacular elk chandelier.

Photograph courtesy Crystal Farm

METALWORK

The art of the smithy has been revived in the last ten years and a new generation of metalworkers has emerged, wedded to the trade not by necessity but by true appreciation of the metal and the method of crafting it. Shiny finishes have no place in rustic homes. The matte black of iron or the chestnut glow of bronze with the imperfections of forging or casting offers the ideal contrast and complement to wood and stone. Chandeliers, sconces, lamps, fireplace accessories, and hardware are all readily available to outfit the well-appointed rustic home.

ABOVE Chris Thomson's hand-forged log holder and fireplace tools illustrate a primitive, Southwestern interpretation of the metal.
Photograph by Peter Vitale

RIGHT A cast bronze fireplace screen made by Peter Fillerup depicts elk on the range.
Photograph by Matt Turley

WALL DÉCOR

Fine art is preferable for primary living spaces—oil paintings of nature (antique or contemporary depending upon the context) are highly desirable and stand alone. On large walls multiples work well: a series of framed prints or a collection of tramp art frames, fishing poles, miniature birch bark canoes, or an arrangement of paddles all fit the bill. This should be the enjoyable part of decorating a rustic home; there are no rules here and almost anything goes.

Taxidermy is de rigeuer, fur on or fur off: moose, deer, elk, or just the antlers. Fish, bear, pheasant—anything huntable is hangable.

ABOVE Rusted Rock is known for its dedication to Adirondack style framing and their imaginative moldings that incorporate all the woods has to offer: twig, bark, stone, moss, pinecones, and fungus. They forage for all of the natural materials they incorporate into their work.
Photograph by Mark Hobson

LEFT This wood deer mount from Crystal Farm has been chiseled in the manner of Black Forest carvings made popular in Bavaria and featured in many rustic homes.
Photograph courtesy Crystal Farm

SOFT GOODS

Finishing a home can be an angst-ridden experience—what fabrics to use, where to use them, etc. These are decisions that could make or break a room. As in any style of home, a successful rustic interior requires a balance to hit the right note in the right place. To stand up to the rugged architecture, designers tend toward heavier, textural answers. Regional preferences play a role in color and pattern choices—the Northeast enjoys bold and vibrant plaids, checks, and geometrical motifs, while the homes of the West follow a more monochromatic course, inspired by Native American ideals honoring nature.

Rugs are typically the starting point for a room. Styles appropriate for the rustic home are those that are not too delicate in pattern and have broad planes of color; Navajos, kilims, antique tribals and Tibetans (ideal for the chunkier yarn used) are good candidates. Animal-skin throw rugs can be tossed in amongst these either to break up or bridge the space between two rugs.

An array of fun, kitschy retro fabrics in cabin and outdoor motifs are available today as are more refined, nature-themed prints for the more upscale home. Geometric and linear patterns lend an informal atmosphere—plaids, stripes, and Indian motifs are good options. Textural fabric plays well against a backdrop of log, timber, and stone: chenilles, corduroy, burlap, and leather being natural preferences.

The top layer of décor should be interesting and provide the grace notes for a room: real and faux fur pillows and throws, animal skins, and colorful blankets: Pendleton, antique Beacon, Hudson Bay, plaid and checked wool are readily available to create a mood. When accessorizing the rustic home, taking the road less traveled leads to success. The homeowner willing to steer away from the obvious and take the time to seek out the unusual will be rewarded with a unique and provocative living experience.

In the late 1800s Pendleton Woolen Mills made blankets and robes for Native Americans called Indian trade blankets. They were used as wearing apparel and a standard for value and credit among the tribes. These blankets became prized for ceremonial use. They are still in production, their vivid color and pattern completely at home in the rustic setting.
Photograph courtesy Pendleton Woolen Mills

LEFT A tufted wool headboard is inset into a yellow birch frame in this restful setting. The bedding features a linen deer print duvet cover, dust skirt with deer skin overlay, and vintage balsam pillow. Designed by Ann Stillman O'Leary.

© Gary Hall Photography

CENTER TOP The author's porch. A vibrant red-and-white vintage awning canvas was used for the cushions on the antique wicker. Rustic appointments such as a rainbow trout trophy, fishing poles, and a twig plant stand filled with antique bocce balls create the informal and inviting mood here.

© Gary Hall Photography

ABOVE The Lord Gore bed from Crystal Farm is an essay in rustic decoration.

Photograph courtesy Crystal Farm

SOURCES

ANTIQUES

Black Bass Antiques
Lake Shore Dr.
Bolton Landing, NY 12814
518-644-2389
henry@blackbassantiques.com

Robert L. Burger Sporting Art and
Antiques
PO Box 765
Mount Vernon, OH 43050
740-392-9101
burger@ecr.net

Cherry Gallery
4 Stissing Mt. Lane
Pine Plains, NY 12567
518-398-7531
info@cherrygallery.com
www.cherrygallery.com

Christiby's
Traverse City, MI
231-947-5906
www.christiby's.com

Brian Correll Antiques
499 North Main St.
Gloversville, NY 12078
518-725-2049
bdcorr@citlink.net

Linda Davidson Antiques
726 East Lakeshore Dr.
Landrum, SC 29356
864-457-5239
davidsons@charter.net
www.adorondack.com

Fern Eldridge Antiques
Rte. 4
Northwood, NH
603-942-5602
fern27@metrocast.net
www.directiques.com

Fighting Bear Antiques
PO Box 3790
Jackson, WY 83001
307 733 2669
fightingbear@onewest.net
www.fightingbear.com

Forest Home Furnishings
141 River St.
Saranac Lake, NY 12983
518-891-6692
vgnap@adelphia.net

Magoun Brothers
125 Ryerson Hill Rd.
So. Paris, ME 04281
207-743-2040

Moose America
2499 Main St.
Rangeley, ME 04970
207-864-3699
bob.mooseamerica@verizon.net

Alan Pereske
2158 Saranac Ave.
Lake Placid, NY 12946
518-891-3733
sapereske@peoplepc.com
www.alanpereskeantiques.com

The Quiet Moose
2666 Charlevoix Ave.
Petoskey, MI 49770
231-348-5353
800-960-0800

Rituals
756 N. La Cienaga Blvd.
Los Angeles, CA 90069
310 854 0848
www.ritualsdecor.com

Shaggy Ram
PO Box 2727
210 Edwards Village Blvd.
Edwards, CO 81632
970-926-7377
theshaggyram@aol.com
www.theshaggyram.com

Simple Life Antiques
PO Box 361
Land O' Lakes, WI 54540
715-547-6666
simplelf@nnex.net
www.simplelifeantiques.com

Ski Country Antiques
114 Homestead Rd.
Evergreen, CO 80439
303-674-4666
jeff@skicountryantiques.com
www.skicountryantiques.com

Sleighbell Antiques
Rte. 4
Northwood, NH 03261
603-942-9988
www.sleighbellantiques.com

ANTLER

Crystal Farm Antler Chandeliers
and Furniture
18 Antelope Rd.
Redstone, CO 81623
970-963-2350
crystalfarm@direcway.com
www.crystalfarm.com

Gone Wild Creations
25 Washington St.
Ellicottville, NY 14731
716-699-6400
gonewild2@aol.com
www.gonewildcreations.com

ARCHITECTS

Robert Bradbury, Architect
141 Hulls Falls Rd.
Keene, NY 12942
518-576-9914
bradiron@kvbi.net

CCY Architects
228 Midland Ave.
Basalt, CO 81621
970-927-4925
info@ccyarchitects.com
www.ccyarchitects.com

CTM Architects
Candace Tillotson-Miller
208 West Park St.
Livingston, MT 59047
406-222-7057
cmiller@ctmarchitects.com
www.ctmarchitects.com

Jack Davis, Architect
321 Pharr Rd. Suite D
Atlanta, GA 30305
404-237-2333
Jacksdavis@networktel.net

Faulkner Architects
Greg Faulkner
12242 Business Park Dr.
Number 18
Truckee, CA 96161
530-582-7400
general@faulknerarchitects.net
www.faulknerarchitects.net

Faure-Halvorsen Architects
1425 W. Main St. Suite A
Bozeman, MT 69715
406-587-1204
fha@faurehalvorsen.com
www.faurehalvorsen.com

Fletcher Farr Ayotte, PC
708 S.W. Third Ave., Suite 200
Portland, OR 97204
503-222-1661
info@ffadesign.com
www.ffadesign.com

Richard Giegengack, AIA
2901 Q Street, NW
Washington, DC 20007
202-338-9531
rgiegengack@msn.com

Greene and Associates
Tim Greene
P.O. Box 827
Canoe Point
Cashiers, NC 28717
828-743-2968
tcpgreene@aol.com

Nils E. Luderowski, AIA
1774 Main St.
Keene Valley, NY 12943-0052
518-576-4446
nel@kvvi.net

Larry E. Pearson Architectural
777 E Main St.
Bozeman, MT 59715-3808
406-587-1997

Peter Pennoyer Architects, PC
432 Park Avenue South
New York, NY 10016
212-779-9765
peter@ppapc.com
www.ppapc.com

Piper/Architecture, LTD
Duane Piper
PO Box 5560
Avon, CO 81620
970-949-7074
dpiper@vail.net

RKD Architects, Jack Snow
137 Main St., Suite G004
Edwards, CO 81632
970-926-2622
snow@rkdarch.com
www.rkdarch.com

SALA Architects, Inc.
Katherine Hillbrand
904 South Fourth St.
Stillwater, MN 55082
651-351-0961
info@salaarc.com
www.salaarc.com

Sellers and Company
David Sellers
P.O. Box 288
Warren, VT 05674
802-496-2787
dave@sellersandcompany.com
www.sellersandcompany.com

Shamburger Design Studio
Wayland Shamburger
118 Ashwood Rd.
Hendersonville, NC 28791
828-692-2737
designstudio@brinet.com

Sheerr and White Residential
Architecture, Deidre Sheerr-
Gross, Peter J. White
224 Main St.
New London, NH 03257
603-526-2445
athome@sheerrwhite.com
www.sheerrwhite.com

Shepherd Resources, Inc/AIA -
Douglas Miller DeChant
37347 US Hwy. 6, Suite 102
Avon, CO 81620
970-949-3302
doug@sriarchitect.com
www.sriarchitect.com

Shope Reno Wharton Associates,
Allan Shope
18 West Putnam Ave.
Greenwich, CT 06830
203-869-7250
jhupy@srwol.com
www.shoperenowharton.com

Elizabeth Stewart Design, LLC,
Elizabeth Stewart and
Reed Morrison
12 East 86th St. #809
New York, NY 10028
212-734-5487
also: PO Box 945
Wainscot, NY 11975
631-537-5768

TAB Associates, Inc., Tab Bonidy
37347 Hwy. 6, Suite 228
Avon, CO 81620
970-748-1470
tab@vail.net
www.tabassociates.com

Christopher P. Williams Architects
4 Stevens Ave.
Meredith, NH 03253-0703
603-279-6513
info@cpwarchitects.com

VAG, Inc. Architects and Planners
PO Box 1734
Vail, CO 81658
970-949-7034
general@vagarchitects.com
www.vagarchitects.com

BUILDERS

Keith Ashe
Ashe Construction Inc.
44 Paisley Mtn.
Cashiers, NC 28717-8613
828-743-6350

Hoover Austin
PO Box 585
Moretown, VT 05660
802-496-3963

Beck Building Company
780 Nottingham Rd.
Avon, CO 81620
970-949-1800
andy@beckbuilds.com
www.beckbuilds.com

Biesmeyer's Adirondack Building
and Contracting, Inc.
Hulls Falls Rd.
Keene, NY
518-576-4210

Bullock Log Homes
12 Greengage Rd.
New Lowell, ON Canada
705-424-5222
bullockloghomes@bellnet.ca
www.bullockloghomes.com

Cascade Builders
128 Pine St.
Saranac Lake, NY 12983
518-891-8123
cascadeuilders@
adelphia.net

Baird Edmonds Builder, Inc.
1774 NYS Route 73
Keene Valley, NY 12943
518-576-4401
bebinc@kvvi.net

Nick Heinen Construction, Inc.
1991 Grand Ave. Apt. #3
St. Paul, MN 55105
612-910-6716
voss1@comcast.net

Peter Holderied
9 Highland Place
Lake Placid, NY 12946
518-523-2781

Landmark Builders
383 Co. Hwy. 112
Gloversville, NY 12078

Luckey and Co.
P.O.Box 2202
Branford, CT 06405
203-481 9780
thomasluckey@aol.com

Maple Island Log Homes
5046 S. West Bayshore Dr.
Suttons Bay, MI 49682
231-271-4042
mail@mapleisland.com
www.mapleisland.com

McGray and Nichols Builders
9 Newport Rd.
New London, NH 03257
603-526-2874

Mulligan and Phillips
55 Monroe Place #408
Bloomfield, NJ 07003
973-748-4680
mulphi@msn.com

Neal and Sweet, LLC
10-12 North Perry St.
PO Box 712
Johnstown, NY 12095
518-562-2115
nsjohn@nycap.rr.com

John Niemann
16341 May Ave. North
Marine on St. Croix, MN 55047
651-433-3794
niemann@juno.com

Northland Design and
Construction
RR100
Waitsfield, VT 05673
802-496-2108

Redwing Construction
250 Averyville Rd.
Lake Placid, NY 12946
518-523-1754

Resort Concepts
37347 US Hwy.6, Suite #206
Avon, CO
970-949-9432

SBE Builders
1700 Post Rd. Suite B-10
Faifield, CT 06824
sbepifano@sbecoinc.com

George Schaeffer Construction Co.
41011 US Hwy 6 & 24
Avon, CO 81620
970-845-5656
george@gsconco.com
www.georgeshaeffer.com

Sitecraft Construction Corp.
PO Box 387
Truckee, CA 96160
pam@sitecraft+cc.com

Tissot Construction Co.
632 County Rte. 47
Saranac Lake, NY 12983
518-891-1645

Trillium Construction
46 Links Dr.
Cashiers, NC 28717
828-743-6147

Whitehouse Construction
6 Lily Pond Rd.
Gilford, NH 03249
603-528-2282

Yellowstone Traditions, Inc.
34290 East Frontage Rd.
Bozeman, MT 59715
406-587-0968
info@yellowstonetraditions.com
www.yellowstonetraditions.com

FURNITURE MAKERS AND WOOD ARTISANS

Beeken-Parsons
Shelburne farms
1611 Harbor Rd.
Shelburne, VT 05482
802-985-2913
info@beekenparsons.com
www.beekenparsons.com

Gary Michael Brewer Custom
Carpentry
PO Box 450
Au Sable Forks, NY 12912
518-647-8819

John Bryan
198 Milliken Rd.
North Yarmouth, ME 04097
jbryan@bryanart.com
www.bryanart.com

Brad Corriveau
59 Dutile Rd.
Belmont, NH 03220
603-524-8780

The Great Camp Collection
PO Box 978
Carbondale, CO 81623
970-963-0786
info@thegreatcampcollection.com
www.thegreatcampcollection.com

Barry Gregson
Adirondack Rustics Gallery
Rte. 9
Schroon Lake, NY 12870
info@adirondackrusticsgallery.com
www.adkrustics.com

Howard Hatch
PO Box 1467
Conway, NH 03818
603 447 8486
hhatch@ncia.net
www.hatchstudio.com

Hawkins Unique Mosaic Twig Art
Furnishings
4621 Markey Rd.
Roscommon, MI 48653
800-838-0208

Highlands Craftsmen
PO Box 2011
Blowing Rock, NC 28605
828-295-0796
chris@highlandcraftsmen.com
www.highlandcraftsmen.com

Icarus Furniture
154 Fourth St.
Troy, NY 12180
518-274-2883
www.icarusfurniture.com

George Jacques
Rte 73
Keene Valley, NY 12943
518-576-2214

Daniel Mack Rustic Furnishings
14 Welling Ave.
Warwick, NY 10990
845-986-7293
rustic@warwick.net
www.danielmack.com

Lionel Maurier
26 Tucker Mountain Rd.
Meredith, NH 03253
603-279-4320

Clifton Monteith
20341 Fowler Rd.
Box 9
Lake Ann, MI 49650
231-275-6560
monteith@centurytel.net
homepage.mac.com/cliftonmonteith

Neal and Sweet, LLC, Jon Sweet
10-12 North Perry St.
PO Box 712
Johnstown, NY 12095
518-762-2115
nsjohn@nycap.rr.com

David Norton
PO Box 91
Kearsarge, NH 03847
603-447-2392

Old Hickory Furniture Co.
403 South Noble St.
Shelbyville, IN 46176
800-232 -BARK
www.oldhickory.com

Sampson Bog Studio
171 Paradise Point
Mayfield, NY 12117
518-661-6563

Sleeping Bear Twig Furniture
5711 Rice Rd.
Cedar, MI 49621
231-228-6633
www.hoffmansweb.com

Mark Smith Timber Framing
281 Littleworth Rd.
Madbury, NH 03823
603-742-1180
mcslog@aol.com

Paul Stark
69705 Lake Dr.
Sisters, OR 97759
541-549-0136 or 514-815-4792

Doug Tedrow
Wood River Rustics
PO Box 3446
Ketchum, ID 83340
208-726-1442

Timpson Creek Gallery
7142 Hwy 76 West
Clayton, GA 30525
706-782-5164
timpsoncrkgallery@alltel.net

Mike Trivieri
Moody Rd.
Tupper Lake, NY 12986
518-359-7151

GLASS

Lyn Hovey Studio, Inc.
1476 River St.
Hyde Park, MA 02136
617-333-9445
officemgr@lynhoveystudio.com
www.lynhoveystudio.com

INTERIOR DESIGNERS

Clark Planning and Design
Mary Clark Conley
470 School St.
Rumney, NH 03266-3423
603-786-3635

Design Coalition, David Krajeski
7045 North SR32
Peoa, UT 80461
435-783-6060

Design Project, Inc.
Chris Stevens
1064 County Road 127
Glenwood Springs, CO 81601
970-384-0092

Gandy/Peace, Peace Design
Incorporated
349 Peachtree Hills Ave.
Suite C-2
Atlanta, GA 30305
404-237-8681

Gomez Associates
Mariette Himes Gomez
504 East 74th St.
New York, NY 10021
877-466- shop (7467)
www.gomezassociates.com

Barbara Hart Interior Design,
Barbara Hart, Pamela Kostmayer
3126 Golf Course Rd.
Owings Mills, MD 21117
410- 581-8118
hartbi@aol.com

Monday's House of Design,
Lynn Monday
Grouse Pt.
Cashiers, NC 28717
828-743-2094

Northpoint Lodge Collection
10472 W. Murphy Blvd.
Hayward, WI 54843
715-462-3793

Greg Pinch
Toronto, Ontario
416-927-9118
greg.pinch@rogers.com

Rogers-Ford, L.C. Architecture-
Design
2616 Thomas Ave.
Dallas, TX 75204
214-871-9388
info@rogers-ford.com
www.rogers-ford.com

Slifer Designs
216 Main St., Suite C-100
Edwards, CO 81632
970-926-8200
info@sliferdesigns.com
www.slifer.com

Ann Stillman O'Leary
(Evergreen House)
2475 Main St.
Lake Placid, NY 12946
518-523-4263
annsoleary@msn.com

Ginny Stine Interiors
Ginny Stine Romano
1936 San Marco Blvd.
Jacksonville, FL 32207
904-396-9814

Travis & Company
351 Peachtree Hills Avenue
Suite 128
Atlanta, GA 30305
404-237-5079

Vallone Design, Donna Vallone,
Caroline DeCesare
7007 East Third Ave.
Scottsdale, AZ 85251
480-421-2799
donna@vallonedesign.com
www.vallonedesign.com

Western Traditions, Vicki Ward
63 Avondale Lane, #C-1
Beaver Creek, CO 81620
970-748-5010

LANDSCAPE

Land Design by Ellison
Glen Ellison, Pam Granade
PO Box 1259
Avon, CO 81620
970-949-1700
info@ldbye.com
www.ldbye.com

LIGHTING

Lean-To Studio
PO Box 222
Adirondack, NY 12808
518-494-5185
mail@lean2.com
www.lean2.com

Dennis Sparling Studio
1435 Quarry Road
New Haven, CT 05472
802-453-4114
www.sparlingstudio.com

METAL ARTISANS

Chicken Coop Forge
992 East River Dr.
Lake Luzerne, NY 12846
518-798-9174

Jim Guy
938 Sylvania Dr.
Dallas, TX 75218
469-624-5203
jguydesign@earthlink.net

Joslyn Fine Metalworks, Inc.
1244 Route 80
Smyrna, NY 13464
607-627-6580
steve@usblacksmith.com
www.usblacksmith.com

Hammerton
2149 S. 3140 W
Salt Lake City, Utah 84119
801-973-8095
info@hammerton.com
www.hammerton.com

Mountain Lighting and Forge
PO Box 279
Cory, CO 81414
866-55forge
wayne@mountainlighting.com
www.mountainlighting.com

Eric Reece
4611 Route 233
Clinton, NY 13323
315-853-7155

Christopher Thomson Ironworks
PO Box 578
Ribera, NM 87560
800-726-0145
christo@plateautel.net
www.christhomsoniron.com

Wild West Designs
Peter Fillerup
577 W. 910 S.
Heber City, UT 84032
435-654-4151
peter@wildwestdesigns.com
www.wildwestdesigns.com

RUGS AND BLANKETS

Bounds Cave Oriental Rugs
Hwy 64E
Cashiers, NC
828-743-5493
boundscave@aol.com
www.mountainshops.com/
boundscave

Barry Friedman
e-mail:blanketboy@cox.net
www.blanketboy.net

Pendleton Woolen Mills
PO Box 3030
Portland, OR 97208-3030
800-760-4844
www.pendleton-usa.com

Tahoe Rug Studio
Cobblestone Center
Tahoe City
530-581-2555

STONE

Lamphere Contracting Corp.
2593 Plank Rd.
Berlin, NY 12022
518-658-3702

McKernon Stone Masonry
Thomas H. McKernon
PO Box 77
Gabriels, NY 12939
518-327-3223
atmckernan@adelphia.net

Stone Age Design, LLC
Chad Sanborn
8 Chipmunk Lane
Gilmanton Ironworks, NH 03837
603-267-6600

STORES

Adirondack Store
109 Saranac Ave.
Lake Placid, NY 12946
518-523-2646
also 90 Main St.
New Canaan, CT 06840

The Birch Store
Rte. 73
Keene Valley, NY 12943
518-576-4561

Gorsuch Limited
263 East Gore Creek Dr.
Vail, CO 81657
Catalog 800-525-9808
www.gorsuchltd.com

High Camp Home
11890 Donner Pass Rd.
Truckee, CA
530-582-6866

Midnight Farms
336 Hwy. 107N
Cashiers, NC
828-743-5858
info@midnightfarms.com
www.midnightfarms.com

Rusted Rock Studio Gallery
Main St.(Rte. 73)
Keene, NY
518-576-9102

Rusticks
32 Canoe Point
Cashiers, NC
828-743-3172

Summer House/Tiger Mountain
Woodworks
Hwy 106-Dillard Rd.
Highlands, NC 28741
828-526-2673

Turkey Mountain Traders
7008 East Main St.
Scottsdale, AZ 85251
480-423 8777
www.turkey-mountain.com

INDEX

Courtesy Ryan Wolffe